Karel Sládek
Tomáš Špidlík
A Theological Life

T0083501

KAROLINUM PRESS
PRAGUE 2019

The manuscript was reviewed by Pavel Ambros (Palacký University Olomouc) and Marek Petro (University of Prešov).

Issued on the occasion of the 100th anniversary of the birth of Professor Tomáš Špidlík (1919–2010).

KAROLINUM PRESS
Karolinum Press is a publishing department of Charles University
Ovocný trh 560/5, 116 36 Prague 1
Czech Republic
www.karolinum.cz

Designed by Zdeněk Ziegler
Set and printed in the Czech Republic by Karolinum Press
First English edition

Cataloguing-in-Publication Data is available from the National Library
of the Czech Republic

ISBN 978-80-246-4379-3
ISBN 978-80-246-4493-6 (pdf)

Karolinum Press

CONTENTS

Only three of the works of Tomáš Špidlík cited in this book have been translated into English. They are: *The Spirituality of the Christian East: A Systematic Handbook*, translated by Anthony Gythiel; *Prayer*, again translated by Gythiel; *The Art of Purifying the Heart*, translated by Liam Kelly.

All quotations from these works are taken from those translations. Quotations from all other works are our own translations.

In the footnotes, to help the reader, we have offered translations of the titles of works published in Czech or Italian. Subsequent short references to these works are based on that English translation.

Pavlina and Tim Morgan

I came to know Tomáš Špidlík while studying philosophy and theology in Rome. I was already familiar with some of his work—I had read *Prameny světla* (Sources of light) and attended some of the lectures he had given in the Czech Republic on Slavic spirituality—but longed to meet him in person. So I called him at the Centro Aletti where he lived and worked, and he happily agreed to a meeting despite my being a complete stranger.

The day came. I rang the bell, passed through the lodge and took the lift up to Špidlík's room. The doors slid open and there was the man himself, come to meet me, wearing his inimitable smile. He wanted to know what I was doing in Rome, what I was studying, and listened attentively as I answered his gentle probing. He in turn told me about his travels, his thoughts on the state of the church and contemporary society in the Czech Republic from his perspective in Rome, and about the spirituality of the Christian East and the great interest some Orthodox theologians were showing in his work in the field of spiritual theology. More visits followed. He was particularly anxious to show me round the art studio and talk to me about the meaning of art, especially depictions of the divine-human face through which artists seek to express a human relationship to the sacred.

In the autumn of 2002, I was privileged to accompany Father Špidlík (as he was then) to Terni in Umbria where he was to speak at a conference entitled "Holiness and charity in the Christianity of East and West," organised by the Community of Sant'Egidio. Among the Catholic and Russian Orthodox theologians taking part was Metropolitan Kirill of Smolensk and Kaliningrad, now patriarch of Moscow and all Russia. Ever the gentleman, Špidlík made a point of striking up conversations with all the speakers, making all he met laugh and smile with his gentle humour; ever the theologian, he never failed to make a profound, erudite, yet humble contribution to the various discussions. In his own lecture on "The Love of the *Starets*: Father Pio of Pietrelcina and Saint John of Kronstadt," he pointed out the similarities in the way holiness manifested itself in these two men. On the final evening, I accompanied Father Špidlík to the station and we sat on the platform talking around some of the themes that interested me as a student of theology. He listened very patiently, always able to come to the crux of whatever we were discussing, and gently pressed me to direct my research more to the matter of holiness than to disputes over the Filioque clause. The train arrived, I helped him on with his luggage, and he left for Rome. I felt calm, composed, and full of joy.

Whenever we met at the Centro Aletti, Špidlík would subtly ask me about my goals in life. If I stumbled over an answer, he would offer a story from his own experience which inevitably related to the questions I was asking myself at the time. The atmosphere was always imbued with humour, always friendly. He was an excellent mentor—truly a *starets* for our times.

My final two memories of Cardinal Tomáš Špidlík (as he became) are from after I had returned to the Czech Republic from my studies in Rome. I had been offered a place to continue my doctoral research at the Catholic Faculty of Charles University in Prague, and as I pondered over the subject of my thesis, I called Špidlík in Rome. He told me he would think about it and that I should call him back in a week's time. When we spoke again, he suggested I study the life and work of the Russian theologian Vladimir Solovyev. And so I did. My final face-to-face encounter with Špidlík took place at a meeting with the academic community in Prague attended by Pope Benedict XVI. Although we managed only the very briefest of conversations, I will never forget how he once again received me very warmly and with his ever-present smile.

In my heart, Tomáš Špidlík will always remain a holy man who had time for friends, was always interested in whatever they were doing and sought what was best for them. I hope this book will go at least some way towards expressing the enormous gratitude I feel for all he did for me.

Karel Sládek, June 2018

Cardinal Tomáš Špidlík SJ (1919–2010) was a distinguished Czech priest and theologian who left a significant mark on the history of the universal Church. His work gained broad respect during his lifetime—and has continued to do so since—as witnessed by the many awards and commendations he received for his contributions to the fields of theology, ecumenism, and culture and the arts. His books are much in demand from Christians of both East and West but have also gained respect among the wider academic community and in the world at large.

The interpretative lens for this particular contribution to the growing literature on Špidlík's life and work is theological. Although the book sketches out the main events that punctuated Špidlík's life, it is not a classical historiography or biography, but a spiritual-theological interpretation of how his theological research was shaped by his life experiences, and vice versa.

Špidlík's principal focus was spiritual theology, in particular a systematic exploration of the relationship between human beings and the triune God on the basis of the human experience of divine revelation. The twin sources of that revelation are Scripture and Church tradition, which for Špidlík meant the tradition of both Western Christianity, especially his own Jesuit spirituality, and the Eastern Church, where his particular interest lay in the Russian religious thinkers.

It will become clear how his growth in wisdom and his profound knowledge of Scripture and of the traditions of the Christian East and West influenced the choices he made both in his life and in his work as a theologian, which were in large part one and the same thing. The approach here is therefore both deductive and inductive. We will show how the theological foci that formed and informed Špidlík's spiritual life, and the inspiration which followed, contributed to the synthesis of his personal and theological life. This synthesis led Špidlík to a new reading of Christian tradition, a tradition he was able to further enrich by means of a "hermeneutic spiral," a constant listening to the Spirit and deepening of his faith. His lifelong work culminated in a series of reflections on the theology of beauty and in giving form to the spirituality of the Centro Aletti where he lived and worked for the final years of his life.

The book is divided into three sections: first, a theological interpretation of Špidlík's life and work; next, an exploration of his theological synthesis of the spirituality of the Christian East and West; and finally, a review of his theological "last will and testament" concerning the theology of art. Individual chapters were written up gradually from the fruit of various lectures and academic colloquia, and then collected, collated and ordered thematically to form the present volume. Some sections have already been published in Czech in edited monographs and other scholarly works. This work collects the various pieces to form a more complete picture of Špidlík's theological legacy.

Tomáš Špidlík's theological output was vast and very broad and what we are now seeing represents only the initial reflections on that legacy—the first swallows of summer. The intention here is not to provide a comprehensive discussion of Špildík's theology or to pass comment on what others have written about it, but simply to present the more significant lines of his thinking as they developed throughout his life. The sources cited are those of Špidlík's works which deal with the issues addressed in the individual chapters; a more detailed analysis of his entire oeuvre must wait another day.

Tomáš Špidlík constantly evaluated his life in light of both the will of God and his own theological reflections, and saw every encounter as an opportunity to consider very carefully the direction his life and his theological research were taking.

In this opening chapter, we will seek a theological interpretation of Špidlík's life by exploring the connections between his life experience and his theological work in three areas: first, how his views on the spirituality of the family grew out of his relationship with his own parents; secondly, how his time at Velehrad in Moravia—a time he saw very much as God's providence and spiritual guidance—prompted him to seek a deeper understanding of the spirituality of the Christian East; and finally, how he reflected on wisdom in many of his writings.

THE FAMILY, AND SPIRITUAL SONHOOD AND FATHERHOOD

Špidlík was born on 17 December 1919 in Boskovice, Czech Republic. After passing his grammar school exams in 1938, he studied Latin and Czech literature at the Faculty of Arts at Masaryk University in Brno. In 1940, he entered the novitiate of the Society of Jesus in Benešov, but soon moved to Velehrad, where during the war years he would complete his studies in philosophy and go on to teach Czech and Russian language at the grammar school.

After the war, he continued his theological studies abroad, first in Maastricht, and then from 1951 onwards in Rome at the Pontifical Institute of Oriental Studies and the Pontifical Nepomuceno Seminary (the old Bohemian seminary), where he became spiritual director to the seminarians.

Špidlík, His Parents, and His Theology of Family

Špidlík wrote and spoke on the spirituality of the family in numerous articles, sermons, interviews and public lectures, and no theological interpretation of his life would be complete without noting how his thoughts on the subject reflected his own experience of family—both his blood family and his spiritual family, the Society of Jesus.

From his early works offering practical and pastoral advice on marriage and family life, Špidlík moved on to deeper, spiritual-theological and often mystical reflections which sought links between the spirituality of familial relationships—husband and wife, father and mother, parent and child, brother and sister—and the mystery of the relationships within the Holy Trinity.

> The life of the Holy Trinity . . . is reflected in the life of the Church, and the life of the Church . . . is reflected in marriage. In the economy of salvation, after a descent there follows an ascent: from marriage, through the Church, to participation in the divine life of the Trinity.[1]

Here is the essence of Špidlík's spirituality of the family. It is based on the revelation of the Holy Trinity, who descends to the human person—father, mother, child—in order to lift that person up into the sacramental life of the Church. We will begin, however, from the opposite, human perspective, from Špidlík's own experience of family, beginning with his recollections of childhood.

> My mother had much to do and largely entrusted me to the care of my sisters, each of them older than me, one by five years and the other by six. They would take me outside where they would chat with other girls, leaving me to play in the middle of the street like some lonely little man.[2]

Špidlík had an eventful childhood but managed to survive a near drowning, a ferocious attack by a pig, and on one memorable occasion a close shave with a speeding carriage. Later in life he would reflect on these dramatic and sometimes amusing events:

> Over the course of my life I have encountered many unexpected dangers, but God has always saved me from them—sometimes in ways that were more unexpected than the events themselves.[3]

1) Tomáš Špidlík, *My v Trojici* [We in the Trinity] (Kostelní Vydří: Karmelitánské nakladatelství, 2000), 93.
2) Tomáš Špidlík, *Duše poutníka. Tomáš Špidlík v rozhovoru s Janem Paulasem* [Soul of a pilgrim: Tomáš Špidlík in conversation with Jan Paulas] (Kostelní Vydří: Karmelitánské nakladatelství, 2004), 17.
3) Ibid.

His experience of the care and protection of God through his childhood years strengthened his faith in providence and guidance. When in the wisdom of old age he thought about his parents, he was able to love and understand them with all their strengths and desire for holiness, but also with their inner struggles and short-comings. He had especially painful memories of his father, who had an "unfortunate" relationship with the rest of the family: "He was always snapping at us, and we little ones would run away from him."[4] Špidlík's mother cared for her husband throughout his long illness; he in return offered little but "harsh words of admonition."[5]

Špidlík tried hard to understand his father and accept his many weaknesses, including a difficult personality caused to some extent by an excessive idealism for which he blamed everyone but himself. He was particularly affected by the Great War, after which he fell out of love with the Church and would criticise Špidlík's mother for her acts of religious devotion. He once visited Tomáš in the no-vitiate with a view to tempting him back to their smallholding, but burst into tears when he realised that his dream of handing down to his son everything he had spent his life working for had come to nothing.

Špidlík recognised both the good he had received from his par-ents and his own struggles against similar temptations. He knew he had inherited his father's tendency to feel misunderstood, and his idealism, but this was always balanced by what he had learned from his mother: "I see clearly now that my mother's whole approach to life can be summed up in a single word: pilgrimage."[6] Špidlík's moth-er was indeed a true pilgrim. A deeply religious person, she saw the whole of life as a journey and loved going on pilgrimages. This view of life as a journey, a spiritual pilgrimage, with unpredictable twists and turns but the sure hope of salvation, would become one of the principal motifs of Špidlík's life. The best-known biography of his life and work is called *Duše poutníka* (Soul of a pilgrim).

Špidlík's experience of childhood and his understanding of him-self as his parents' son are intimately connected with his theological

4) Ibid., 18.
5) Ibid., 20.
6) Ibid.

reflections on the family. This was a mutually enriching process—his experiences provided the basis for his reflections, which in turn and in retrospect helped him understand his experience of family.

Špidlík's primary theological focus was the doctrine of the Holy Trinity. In his vision of the family, the different expressions of the persons of the Holy Trinity are revealed, symbolically, in the various roles of the family members: father, mother, children.

> The father is indeed a natural image of God the Father: he is the source of all initiative, directing everyone's labour and their attitudes. Children generally do what they see their parents doing, and are therefore an image of the Son of God; the mother is the love that holds everyone together and is therefore a reflection of the Holy Spirit.[7]

Elsewhere, he considers the same idea but with a different outcome:

> The father of the family is an image of God the Father; the mother is an image of the Son; the children, born out of the love between the father and the mother, are an image of the Holy Spirit.[8]

Špidlík goes on to appeal to John Chrysostom, for whom the division into the sexes was clearly an initiative of God, unlike other divisions, which are caused by sin. The creation of man and woman was immediately followed by the spiritual union of marriage, which thus becomes a reflection of divine love. Vladimir Solovyev saw the state of being in love, especially young love, as an image of the love of God; likewise, Špidlík considered "the other person [in a relationship] worthy of complete respect, while being aware that one's own development depends on a faithful and intimate relationship with that person in an indissoluble union."[9]

Marriage therefore reflects a higher reality, it is sacramental: married partners sanctify each other. If married life is to reach its full "Trinitarian" potential, a couple will need to fast and pray. Sexual

7) Tomáš Špidlík, *K vyšším věcem jsem se narodil* [I was born for higher things] (Prague: Alverna, 1991), 185.
8) We in the Trinity, 85.
9) Ibid., 83.

abstinence will also bring health and healing and will draw married partners into an awareness of the universal, unifying dimension of love: "Marriage is a sacrament for the realisation of the unity of humanity. In this it resembles the Church."[10]

Špidlík notes that this pivotal intuition of the Catholic Church on the subject of marriage did not appear until after the Second Vatican Council. The Conciliar fathers had originally held the primary purpose of marriage to be procreation, but this notion was completely abandoned in favour of marriage as the realisation of the spiritual unity of the human race. Horizontal and vertical unities are both at play here. Horizontal in the sense of the unity of the generations, whereby "a man and a woman are the children of their parents and are themselves the parents of their posterity."[11] At the same time, when these two people who are not from the same family are united they become "one body" through sanctification in the spiritual vertical.

Špidlík's own experience of childhood and adolescence made him only too aware of the challenges of family life. Later, as a spiritual guide, he would become familiar with the many problems and crises within families and marriages, often caused by the selfishness of either collectivism or individualism. For Špidlík, it was these seemingly conflicting but equally damaging ideologies which lay behind the difficulty young people had in accepting the indissolubility of the marriage union. As we have already noted, in its realisation of unity, marriage resembles the Church, but Špidlík also likened the sacrament of marriage to the sacrament of priesthood:

A priest's task is to build up the mysterious body of Christ, the Church, to preserve its supernatural life, power and unity in the Holy Spirit. A spouse's task is to preserve, maintain and cultivate the natural life of the marital union.[12]

The ultimate model of sacramental, familial love is the Holy Family, and husband and wife should foster a desire to participate

---

10) Tomáš Špidlík, *Klíč k neznámému* [Key to the unknown] (Rome: Křesťanská akademie, 1969), 201.
11) Ibid.
12) Ibid., 203.

in the holiness of God as revealed in the earthly trinity of Joseph, Mary and Jesus. This mirror of the Holy Family enables the couple to recognise in themselves the thorn of original sin and the need for purification from selfish and egoistic inclinations. In his early work, Špidlík held up just such a confessional mirror for couples, writing very practically about the spirituality of family and offering a list of vices against which they should launch a spiritual struggle:

> The sins most common in married life are rudeness, insults, hatred, jealousy and suspicions, arguments, seeking one's independence, frequent entertaining outside the family circle, mismanagement of the family's assets, favouritism towards the relatives of one partner over those of the other, dragging children and relatives into marital disputes, complaining to other people, deception and secretiveness, unfaithfulness.[13]

For Špidlík, the family is "the natural root from which new human roots grow. It is also the most natural environment for healthy human development and for physical, psychological and moral fulfilment."[14]

Špidlík also offered advice on choosing a life partner. Beauty, affection and attraction all have a part to play, he suggested, but should not be the overwhelming focus as such "sympathies" can be temporary, fleeting even. Because couples tend to move quite swiftly from "being in love" towards the beginnings of a true lifelong friendship, their greatest concern should be whether their personalities are complementary. They should also bear in mind their respective religious or denominational inclinations, their economic backgrounds, the future good of any children, and the advice of parents and friends.

On parenthood, Špidlík suggests that parents accept children as a gift from God, that mothers breastfeed their babies, that mother and father share equal responsibility in raising their children, that parents should encourage their children to be good, to pray, to work hard and to lead a moral life, that parents should continue to love

---

13) Tomáš Špidlík, *Po tvých stezkách* [In your footsteps] (Rome: Křesťanská akademie, 1968), 210.
14) Ibid., 208.

their children during the difficult teenage years, should bring them up as individuals, punish them only justly and never in anger, and should provide them with the means to lead an independent life. In return, children have a duty to respect their parents in obedience to the fifth commandment, to honour their authority—provided the parents have not abused it—and to care for parents who are old or infirm.

As with the sins against marriage, Špidlík holds up a confessional mirror for children, especially in the matter of respect for their parents, which he sees as the realm where sin is most prevalent:

> . . . rebellion, unruliness, hatred, ceasing to have contact with their parents, disinterest in their parents' problems, speaking badly about them, criticising them in front of others, being harsh about their faults, or likewise using their parents' weaknesses for their own selfish gain, lording it over them, being ashamed of parents who are poor and uneducated.[15]

On Spiritual Family and Spiritual Fatherhood and Sonhood

Špidlík's experience of family continued among the Jesuits, where his life was guided by the principles of spiritual sonhood and fatherhood. He became a much sought-after confessor and used his experience of spiritual fatherhood in his many essays on the spiritual life, for which he drew heavily on the Jesuit tradition and his study of the Church Fathers and Russian authors. His erudition and his ability to synthesise a range of teachings, drawing together perspectives on spiritual accompaniment from the theologies of East and West, masterfully blending his Ignatian experience with Russian spirituality and the Hesychast mystical tradition, made him truly a spiritual father of the whole Church.

But he was first and foremost a faithful spiritual son of Ignatius of Loyola, and Ignatian exercises would become his lifelong spiritual practice. He first encountered the three-day exercises as a student and would go on to lead them for priests and seminarians at the Nepomuceno in Rome. Although he admitted "it was not at all easy for a novice to appear in front of such critical listeners,"[16] the gift of

---

15) Ibid., 213.
16) Soul of a pilgrim, 150.

spiritual fatherhood began to blossom in his life. To make progress on a journey towards perfection, Špidlík maintained, a Christian needs both an accomplished spiritual father and a genuine experience of spiritual sonship:

> To perform spiritual exercises well, it is not enough only to discover harmony with "the order of creation"—one must enter a dialogue with the Creator himself. And the means of achieving this is consistent with the purpose: through a dialogue with a spiritual father on earth, we are led to a dialogue with God, the heavenly Father.[17]

According to the tradition of both the Russian *starets* and the Ignatian spiritual exercises, true spiritual sonship is experienced as a loving friendship, a sharing of hearts. Spiritual sons are to develop an attitude of obedience towards their spiritual father and to trust his guidance. Špidlík was convinced of this need for a spiritual guide, but how to find one?

> Indeed, the great reputation of the "spiritual fathers," "abbots" and *staretses* of monasticism arose from the discovery that the ability to interpret the will of God for others is not universal; we do not find the gift of prophecy in everyone.[18]

Špidlík's commentary on the longer, four-week Ignatian exercises drew deeply on the thinkers of the Christian East, especially of the patristic period; he also made frequent reference to the Russian spiritual authors. Week one of the exercises is devoted to the disciple's own sinful state, to an honest examination of one's conscience, and to coming, step by step, to true self-knowledge. Using extracts from Pavel Florensky's *The Pillar and Ground of the Truth*, especially the references to Molotovilov's "sensual experience" and his description of the torments of hell, Špidlík encouraged his students to look at their sins from the perspective of eternity, and to repent.[19] He also drew on the reflections of Joseph of Volokolamsk, who being deeply

---

17) Tomáš Špidlík, *Ignác z Loyoly a spiritualita Východu* [Ignatius of Loyola and the spirituality of the East] (Velehrad: Refugium, 2001), 15.
18) Ibid.
19) Ibid., 92–94.

aware of the woes of the world also issued a clear call to repentance.[20] Week two is a meditation on the kingly power of Christ as revealed in his earthly life and ministry, on the Eastern vision of Christ Pantocrator, and on the Incarnation and the life of the Holy Trinity.[21] Week three aims to develop compassion for the suffering Christ, a Christ stripped of his power and glory; in Eastern theology, *kenosis*, abasement, is the very ground of Christ's victory over evil.[22] The fourth and final week is a meditation on the "descent into hell" and the revelation of Christ and his presence in the Church—themes commonly depicted in icons.[23]

Špidlík was always mindful of the need to adapt spiritual exercises not only to his students, which he managed with great spiritual genius, but also to his own ability and experience. He often found his students lacking the ability to discern their thoughts, but spiritual sons need to be able to reveal their thoughts to their spiritual guide if he is to offer the desired help and guidance. Spiritual sonship involves coming to know oneself, reviewing and recapping the state of one's heart, and discovering God's providence and guidance.[24]

Špidlík speaks much of the heart, using the word in its symbolic meaning as a synonym for spirituality. Here he draws on the thinking of Theophan the Recluse, for whom the heart is a great treasury of spiritual, mental and physical emotions,[25] and of Pavel Florensky, who saw the heart as the natural "core" of the spiritual life, through which one comes to know one's thoughts and emotions.[26] Recognising the difference between good and evil thoughts requires "attention to the heart" and careful discernment, and a spiritual son is able to identify both; an impure heart is a "veritable nest of negative passions":

---

20) Ibid., 96.
21) Ibid., 107–115.
22) Ibid., 138.
23) Ibid., 147.
24) Soul of a pilgrim, 150–156.
25) Tomáš Špidlík, *Ruská idea: Jiný pohled na člověka* [The Russian idea: A different view of man] (Velehrad: Refugium, 1996), 272.
26) Tomáš Špidlík, *Prameny světla* [Sources of light] (Velehrad: Refugium, 2005), 309.

Pseudo-Macarius tells us an impure heart is full of thorns and briars, a hiding place for snakes and dragons, a home for Satan himself, a polluted spring which releases its foul water. Crystal clear water is sullied even by dust. But the dark mud at the bottom of the wellspring of the human soul, of which the old water stinks, is given three names by spiritual writers: selfishness, wilfulness, hatred.[27]

In any dialogue with an evil thought, however engaging that dialogue may be, it is vital to remain alert and not to become tired and succumb to the whisperings of the Evil One or agree with the sin that is seeking to take hold of the mind and the will. The ancient monks proposed five stages by which an evil thought penetrates the heart: (1) an initial suggestion or evil image that has the potential to lead us into sin; (2) a conversation with this intrusive image or idea; (3) a struggle against the chains of an impure imagination; (4) consent, and performance of the evil act; and (5) the birth of a lasting "passion" and the constant inclination to evil.[28] Špidlík suggests an attentive heart is able to reject the intrusion of the sinful image or idea during any of the first three stages, and that according to Evagrius, the root, the source of the eight passions that assail the human heart—gluttony, lust, avarice, anger, despondency, despair, vainglory, pride—is egoistic self-love. Remaining vigilant and guarding the heart against evil thoughts requires diligent study of the Scriptures and constant "praying to Jesus" using the "prayer of the heart." A successful spiritual struggle against evil thoughts leads to a state of *apatheia* in which a person finds freedom from the passions, regards them as "laughable" even, and dwells in the joy and love of God. *Apatheia* is not merely a passionless state of unfeeling apathy, however, but the inner strength of the resurrection of the soul. Drawing on John Climacus, Špidlík writes:

> For the person who has reached *apatheia*, the choice of good is easy and joyful. It corresponds to the strength of the pure soul. Strong youngsters rejoice when they can fight against the weakest, and when they are

27) Ibid., 287–288.
28) Tomáš Špidlík, *The Art of Purifying the Heart*, trans. Liam Kelly (Miami: Convivium Press, 2010), 23–27 (original title: *L'arte di purificare il cuore*).

attacked they laugh. Faced with evil thoughts that come into the mind, the free person experiences a similar joy. He/she laughs at such thoughts and has no fear of coming away from them perturbed.[29]

This state of inner peace and calm, much sought by hermits, is a "consuming fire" of love. It is not, therefore, a goal, but part of a process of purification:

> The soul is master of its thoughts at the point where it can use one of them to drive out another, as one drives out "a nail with a nail". . . . Finally, because one's state of prayer is like a "barometer of the spiritual life," there is proof of dispassion when one prays "without distractions," when "the spirit begins to see its own light."[30]

Such authentic but uncommon calm is a sign that often accompanies the discovery of God's will, of one's vocation. When Špidlík's students sought his opinion on their calling to the priesthood, he would counsel patience: discernment is a process, and certainty of any calling would grow over time.

> If someone told me he had always wanted to be a priest, I would usually respond with scepticism: many like those have come and not endured. I, on the other hand, did not want to be a priest, and hold on only through the help of God. It is clear, however, that eventually one needs to arrive at a decision. . . . I would advise them not to make too much of how they felt in the first year. The changes that took place at the Nepomuceno were sometimes so unexpected that they caused chaos even in the soul. By the second year, however, the candidate should have the warm feeling in his heart that he is in the right place, one not chosen by him but a place to which he was called by God. But if he does not reach that point, then such a young man is now losing valuable time—time which could be used for finding his place in life elsewhere.[31]

29) Ibid., 40.
30) Tomáš Špidlík, *The Spirituality of the Christian East: A Systematic Handbook*, trans. Anthony Gythiel (Collegeville, MN: Liturgical Press, 2008), 277 (original title: *La spiritualité de l'Orient chrétien*).
31) Soul of a pilgrim, 53-54.

Spiritual fatherhood goes hand in hand with brotherly admonishment, as living life in common requires mutual correction and the rectification and restitution of those who have sinned. Here, Špidlík's reflections again draw on the works of Joseph of Volokolamsk, for whom the practice of brotherly admonishment was central to a community's ability to praise God with one heart and one voice. But proper admonishment requires sound judgement, which in turn requires profound knowledge of the Scriptures. Admonishment is a service of love:

> The first form of brotherly love, John Chrysostom said, is "to be concerned with one's brothers and to pay attention to their salvation." And "because God has arranged it in this manner, that men be corrected by men," the monks viewed the correction of those who had sinned as an act of charity.[32]

Through his spiritual father, the person being admonished knows that the love of God the Father is active and speaking through the one who admonishes, whose words are for the brother's good and will set him back on the path of salvation. A sense of confusion on the part of the one being admonished indicates that they had succumbed to the offending passion willingly; the absence of any such unrest suggests that they had been drawn in unconsciously.

Špidlík counted the counsel of a spiritual father among the seven gifts of the Holy Spirit:

> A counsellor does not press an issue by force but allows one to see that a thing is better this way or that way. So also with the "other Counsellor," the Holy Spirit. The Pharisees imposed God's law as an external rule and ruthlessly demanded that others observe it. The Apostle understood that such observance of the law does not sanctify, that it is a violence. . . . Saint Paul explains to the Galatians that external obedience to the law is for those whose relationship to God is one of slavery. But the Christian receives into their heart the Spirit who calls out "*Abba*, Father"; they are no longer slaves but sons (Gal 4:6–7).[33]

32) *Systematic Handbook*, 165.
33) Tomáš Špidlík, *Znáš Boha Otce i Syna i Ducha svatého?* [Do you know God the Father, and the Son, and the Holy Spirit?] (Velehrad: Refugium, 2005), 155.

It is the Holy Spirit, then, who leads the spiritual father to an awareness that the Creator is at work in the one being accompanied and is helping that person find their life's calling. Špidlík noted the apparent paradox that God both respects our freedom and "counsels" our heart and conscience regarding how to live the Christian life and follow the path of holiness. He also recalled that Mary, the Mother of God, whose "yes" led to her becoming the immaculate Mother of the Saviour, is also "the Mother of good counsel."[34]

A spiritual father must never stand between a person and God. Rather than talking at length about God, he should seek God's activity in that person's life and introduce him or her to the mystery of the life of the Trinity:

> In my opinion, the greatest temptation for zealous priests lies in desperately seeking to "lead young people in the right path." Few are those who in contact with the other pray, "Lord, enlighten me that I may know where you yourself are leading this person."[35]

In spiritual accompaniment, guide and guided alike are drawn by the Holy Spirit into the life of the Trinity:

> A key element of spiritual life is initiation into the life of God and, equally, the elimination of every obstacle that would prevent the life of God from developing within us and the removal of the chasm between our nothingness and the immense sublimity of God. In Ignatius of Loyola's visions of the Trinity, Jesus Christ appears as the intermediary between people and the Holy Trinity.[36]

Špidlík frequently drew his readers into the mystery of the Trinity manifested in the life of the Christian community through the states of marriage, chastity, and also of friendship. All these forms of human relationship are, or should be, characterised by fidelity, indissolubility, self-sacrifice, and finding strength and joy in the bonds of love. The path to perfection is Trinitarian in character, as the Trinity is reflected and revealed in a person's inner being:

34) Ibid.
35) Soul of a pilgrim, 55.
36) We in the Trinity, 21.

Languages distinguish three personal forms: I, you, and he/she/it. From the perspective of psychological development, the order is more properly I, he/she/it, you. A child's attention is initially focused exclusively on its own self. The child seeks to take possession of external things and assert ownership of them: "This is mine!" When their intelligence begins to awaken, they assume an "objective" attitude to external things. They ask, "What is it?" Yet subconsciously they detect a division between "I" and "it" and try to overcome this distinction. It is very interesting to observe how they achieve this. They do not seek simply to take hold of "it"; rather they personalise it, speaking to this object they know intimately and calling it "you."[37]

In *Monasticism*, volume four of *The Spirituality of the Christian East*, Špidlík offers a summary of the characteristics of a spiritual guide. First, they are fathers who lead others to participate in the fatherhood of God; they are prompted by the Holy Spirit, who speaks through them; they can be lay or ordained, male or female—spiritual fathers or mothers; they have the gift of *diakrisis*, the discernment of thoughts; they have the gift of prophecy—they are spiritually articulate; they are good, yet firm.[38]

Chief among the charisms of a spiritual father—and here Špidlík is thinking especially of the Russian *starets*—is *cardiognosis* or knowledge of the heart. A *starets* sees every person as unique and in possession of a unique calling. *Cardiognosis* provides insight into a person's inner state and their relationship with God; it confers knowledge of both the goodness of the soul and the burden of sin:

What was so impressive about the *starets*es was their *cardiognosis* or *proairesis*, their gift of discernment. . . . Ambrose from the monastery at Optina could "read a soul as though it were a book." A visitor might be very quiet, or hidden behind other people, but the *starets* knew his life, the state of his soul, and why he had come to Optina. Not wishing to divulge his gift of discernment he would ask the visitor questions, but

37) Ibid., 105.
38) Tomáš Špidlík, *Spiritualita křesťanského Východu*, vol. 4, *Mnišství* [The spirituality of the Christian East: Monasticism] (Velehrad: Refugium, 2004), 103-104.

the way he asked those questions clearly demonstrated that he already knew everything there was to know.[39]

These rules of spiritual accompaniment demonstrate Špidlík's obvious desire to be faithful to the spiritual heritage of his "other family," the Society of Jesus, to conscientiously live out his vocation as a spiritual father, and to integrate this vocation with his creative work in the field of theology and the dialogue between the Christian East and West.[40]

THE THEOLOGIAN WITH THE "SPIRIT OF VELEHRAD"

The tradition and heritage of Velehrad, the most significant symbol in the Czech Republic of the encounter between Eastern and Western Christianity, was personified in the life and work of Tomáš Špidlík. His wish to be buried at Velehrad testifies to his having been faithful to his vocation and to his efforts for Christian unity to the very end. On the day of his funeral, his coffin was placed in the chapel of the Mother of Christian Unity, where it rested beneath the icon of the Mother of Unity, an icon Špidlík referred to often in his writings. His final resting place is a sarcophagus behind the main altar in the Basilica of the Assumption of the Virgin Mary and Saints Cyril and Methodius.

Velehrad and Its Early Mission

Since the renovation of the basilica in the second half of the nineteenth century and the Unionist congresses at the beginning of the twentieth, Velehrad has very much had its *genius loci* as a meeting place for the Latin and Byzantine rites, a sense of place that is now strengthened by the "presence" of Tomáš Špidlík.

Špidlík was very conscious of the events and encounters that co-created his life and of what they meant for the story of his life with God—"The inter-connection of everything one has experienced offers a foretaste of eternal life"[41]—and he saw that story, his story,

---

39) Russian idea, 142-143.
40) Pavel Ambros, *Kardinal Tomáš Špidlík SJ - starec a teolog nerozdělené církve. Kompletní bibliografie 1938-2011* [Cardinal Tomáš Špidlík SJ: Starets and theologian of an undivided church. A complete bibliography 1938-2011] (Velehrad: Refugium, 2012), 5-95.
41) Soul of a pilgrim, 49.

as being imbued with the "spirit of Velehrad." In 2007, at the celebrations for the centenary of the first Unionist congress, Špidlík said of the congresses:

> It is beyond doubt that their influence reached as far as Rome. They were the catalyst for establishing the Collegium Russicum for seminarians from the East. Also from Velehrad came calls for the foundation of the Pontifical Oriental Institute.[42]

Špidlík was eventually made a professor at the institute—the first Czech priest to be honoured with such a role—and there he continued his research into the dialogue between the spiritualities of the Christian East and West. A copy of the Mother of Unity icon also graced a new altar at the Nepomuceno, where Špidlík had become spiritual director to the seminarians.

> The Velehrad Madonna was created by Professor Dítě and based on the well-known *Salus Populi Romani* Madonna venerated in the church of Santa Maria Maggiore in Rome. The image was to replace the ancient Mother of God icon destroyed during the Hussite uprisings. A legend concerning the original Velehrad monastery suggests it was there that Cyril and Methodius, apostles to the Slavs, dedicated the baptised Slavic nations to the Mother of God so that they may live under her protection in love and unity. . . . The idea of Christian unity would arise again and again.[43]

It is no co-incidence that the Pontifical Institute and the Centro Aletti where Špidlík lived and worked are very close to the church of Santa Maria Maggiore. The legacy of Velehrad thus accompanied him from the very beginning of his spiritual journey, through his novitiate and onto Rome, and from there back to his final resting place.

Špidlík's relationship with Velehrad began during the war when he was still a factory worker. His friend Bohuslav Janíček invited him on a weekend cycling trip to the monastery, where Janíček was

---

42) Tomáš Špidlík, "Cyril a Metoděj: Světci stále aktuální" [Cyril and Methodius: Saints for today], in *Acta VIII. Conventus Velehradensis Anno 2007* (Olomouc: Refugium Velehrad-Roma, 2011), 81.
43) Tomáš Špidlík, "Matka unie" [Mother of Unity], *Nový život* 3 (1954): 37.

seeking to join the Jesuits. On the Sunday, Špidlík was standing by the fountain waiting for his friend to return from an interview when he was spotted by an elderly priest—who turned out to be the rector of Velehrad—and invited to lunch.

> On the way to lunch and after lunch we became so engrossed in conversation that I returned to Velehrad a week later, this time on my own. I had a long conversation with four other priests and later I too was admitted to the Jesuits.[44]

Špidlík entered the novitiate at Benešov near Prague, but very soon the occupying German authorities closed Benešov and moved everyone to Velehrad. It was an intervention that would radically alter the course of Špidlík's spiritual journey and open a new spiritual horizon of the Eastern Christian tradition and liturgy, especially the Cyrillo-Methodian tradition:

> For me, coming to Velehrad also meant a spiritual change. I was touched by the gentle breeze of the Cyrillo-Methodian spirit, which even found its way into some of my poetry: "Oh, resound you joyous song, there where Mojmír's Moravian dreams of bygone glory, where Cyril's holy words cast their final farewell into the bell's heart." Actually it was not a propitious time for such a poem as the Germans were in the process of turning the Velehrad bell into canons for their army.[45]

> One of our fathers who celebrated the Eastern liturgy came to Velehrad. I had just learned to sing it so we celebrated it together. I liked this liturgy very much, right from the start.[46]

The spiritual legacy of Saints Cyril and Methodius was an integral part of the Velehrad tradition and one Špidlík came to know well from the early days of his novitiate and would refer to often in later life, at congresses in Rome, Thessalonica and Ohrid. For Špidlík, this tradition meant a return to the roots of the undivided

44) Soul of a pilgrim, 33.
45) Ibid., 36.
46) Ibid., 37.

Church and the discovery of everything its members hold in common. Czech writings about the "Apostles to the Slavs" were often strongly flavoured with nationalism, especially regarding the Czech language. Špidlík did not feel this inappropriate but pointed out that as Christians we long to go deeper: "Cyril and Methodius established Slavic literature and the Slavic liturgy so that we may better praise God and better understand each other when we pray together. This agenda is forever relevant."[47]

In the mission of Cyril and Methodius, a mission of unity carried out during the break-up of the Roman Empire, Špidlík saw the mission of the Slavic nations. The brothers from Salonica had sought to convince Rome that the Slavs were the people who could provide the necessary bridge between the two Christian cultures. All too soon, however, the Slavs themselves became divided into Western and Eastern, Latin and Byzantine, and the dream was lost.[48] For Špidlík, this mission felt like an invitation from God. He saw in it the largely forgotten "messianic" vocation of the Slavs which began to manifest itself in the West through the Velehrad Unionist congresses and in the East through Russian messianism. The reconciliation offered by the Slavic mission is based on a unity that is personal, lived, Christological and Trinitarian;[49] we will return to this theme later.

Špidlík felt a special spiritual bond with Saint Cyril, whom he compared to the theologian Gregory of Nazianzus. He had a close spiritual affinity with both Cyril and Gregory, and they would become his spiritual and intellectual models. Špidlík studied their theology and their inner lives with great diligence. Their concern for reflection and the contemplative life, their desire for true wisdom and their commitment to being a servant of the Word of God and through that Word to serving their nation was a vocation, a mission, which truly inspired him. Špidlík was equally admiring of Saint

47) Tomáš Špidlík, "Ekumenismus v CM tradici" [Ecumenism in the Cyrillo-Methodian tradition], *Nový život* 7 (1988): 123.

48) Tomáš Špidlík, "Duchovní jednota Evropy" [Spiritual unity in Europe], *Revue Universum* 2 (2004).

49) Tomáš Špidlík, "L'idea cirillo-metodiana e il messianismu slavo: un 'antinomia originaria'?" [The Cyrillo-Methodian idea and the Slavic mission: An 'antinomia originaria'?], *La Civiltà Cattolica* 143 (1992): 431–440.

Methodius, especially of his courage to travel to Rome to explain and defend the brothers' Slavic mission.[50]

Research and Work at the Pontifical Oriental Institute

Špidlík began his theological studies in Maastricht, Holland, and was ordained priest on 22 August 1949. Unable to return to his home country after the arrival of the Communists—the second totalitarian regime to occupy the country in a decade—he continued his Jesuit training in Florence, and from there, in 1951, became spiritual director at the Nepomuceno in Rome, where he was immediately presented with a class of eager seminarians seeking to discern their vocation, and well and truly launched into the world of spiritual fatherhood.

Špidlík stayed at the Nepomuceno until 1989. During his time there he would go for lunch once a week at the Pontifical Oriental Institute, founded in 1917 by Pope Benedict XV for the study of Eastern Christianity and for priests receiving formation as missionaries to the countries of the Christian East and the Islamic world. Talking with the other teachers there, Špidlík felt drawn to obtain his licentiate and doctorate at the Institute, which he succeeded in doing in 1954, defending a thesis on Joseph of Volokolamsk. Špidlík thus continued a great tradition of Czech graduates and teachers from the Institute, such as the Jesuit pioneers Bohumil Horáček and Josef Olšr, who forged strong links with the Russian Orthodox Church and even, despite the many challenges, enabled Russian Orthodox priests to study there. Other Czechs who taught at the Institute included Jan Řezáč, Josef Vaněčka, Jan Krajcar and Jiří Novotný.[51]

The way the Christian West viewed and taught the spirituality of the Christian East was influenced very strongly by the Second Vatican Council, and Špidlík's contribution to this transformation was significant. He originally taught Eastern spirituality in the classic Western style with its division into asceticism and mysticism, but after Vatican II he began presenting the subject as a synthesis of

---

50) Cyril and Methodius: Saints for today, 83-92.
51) Tomáš Špidlík, "Čeští jezuité a slovanský Východ" [Czech Jesuits and the Slavic East], in *Velehrad - filologoi versus filosofoi: Příspěvek spirituální teologie k 800letému výročí* [Velehrad: Philology versus philosophy. A contribution from spiritual theology to the 800th anniversary], ed. Michal Altrichter (Olomouc: Refugium, 2005), 245-249.

the broader spirituality of the Christian East. Špidlík was a great admirer of Russian authors: Theophan Zatvornik (Theophan the Recluse), Fyodor Dostoyevsky, Vladimir Solovyev, Aleksey Khomyakov, Semyon Frank, Nikolai Berdyaev, Sergei Bulgakov, Vyacheslav Ivanov, Lev Shestov, father and son Nikolai and Vladimir Lossky, and Andrei Tarkovsky. Although he was initially discouraged from studying these writers—and encouraged rather to focus on the Armenian church—he returned via the Byzantine origins of spirituality to the Slavic legacy, where his "personal interest focused especially on the prayer of the heart and the priority of freedom over absolute necessity."[52]

Špidlík always understood the global reach of the Christian message, and his passion for a new synthesis of the spirituality of Western and Eastern Christianity was always connected with his concern for the evangelisation of new nations and the missionary task of presenting a Christianity grounded in unity:

> One of the senior authorities in the Orthodox Church asked me why I became interested in Eastern spirituality. I answered more or less this: We cannot close our eyes to the fact that today the so-called Christian world is shifting from Europe to elsewhere. What we are witnessing is something similar to that which took place at the end of Antiquity and with the fall of the old Roman Empire. New "barbarian" nations were becoming Christian and it was necessary to transmit to them a synthesis of the "teaching of the Fathers." Today we are called to transmit to the Christians of Asia and Africa a synthesis of that which is truly Christian from that which Europe gave to the world. But we are yet to express this synthesis. Coming from the centre of Europe, I thank God for having been able to contribute to this task somehow. . . . My assessment was viewed favourably and His Holiness gave me his blessing, just as I had received a blessing from His Holiness in Rome.[53]

This search for a new synthesis of the heritage of Eastern and Western Christianity was crucial for Špidlík. His four volumes of *The Spirituality of the Christian East* contain unique insights into

52) Soul of a pilgrim, 86.
53) Ibid., 81–82.

the many themes of spiritual theology. His methodology reveals not only his rigorous study of patristics and his obvious erudition, but also his profound knowledge of how the Holy Spirit operated through his writings. That the promotion of church unity was truly a spiritual task for Špidlík is partly attested to by the sheer volume of his reflections on the subject, especially in *Ruská idea* (The Russian idea), in which he addresses the mission of the Slavic nations as a bridge between the Christian East and West. His starting point is personalism, with its focus on a "person" who is capable of loving freely in a spirit of self-sacrifice. This principle of a person in the relationships of self-giving that form the basis of relationships in the Church is Christological in nature: God became flesh and offers his Spirit as a gift. In this free co-operation—this *synergeia*—with the Holy Spirit, the human person becomes united with the Holy Trinity through theosis, or deification, and thus holds the key to the resolution of every kind of conflict. In relationships of love, human beings are utterly free, and in love come to know the all-unifying truth which is tangible, creative, intuitive and spiritual—the truth which truly lives. The term the Russians developed for this unity in the Church, for the process by which God's people become united in loving relationships, was *sobornost*. The concept was reflected upon at the Second Vatican Council and provided the inspiration for part of the Dogmatic Constitution on the Church *Lumen gentium* (Light of the nations). Špidlík noted that "the striving for perfection in relationships among people in the Church was expressed at the congress by the term *collegiality*."[54]

Špidlík insisted that the essential ingredient of Church unity was prayer,[55] and wrote about this more mystical aspect of unity in the face of certain Orthodox attitudes towards ecumenism:

> The Orthodox endorse the rule "there is no salvation outside the Church," but none of them admits that all non-Orthodox would be forever condemned. If they are not condemned, they too belong in a certain way to the true Church of Christ.[56]

54) Tomáš Špidlík, *Duše Ruska s Tomášem Špidlíkem* [The Russian soul: A conversation with Tomáš Špidlík] (Kostelní Vydří: Karmelitánské nakladatelství, 2000), 65.
55) Russian idea, 125.
56) Ibid., 128.

Christian unity reaches perfection through a journey of mutual enrichment. The Russians did not downplay the historicity of the Church or the significance of the communion of saints for the unity and final transformation of the Church into eschatological perfection, but stressed that human beings should put this all-unity into practice during this life. Špidlík made a careful study of the Russian thinkers and sought to bring their insights on ecumenism into the life of the universal Church. He felt free to make friends among the Orthodox, to seek co-operation, build bridges, open a dialogue. He reminded his readers and listeners of the "forgotten" mission of the Slavic nations and the importance of coming to know this "all-unity," founded on the unity of the Holy Trinity.

On Ecumenism (or How to Breathe with Both Lungs)

In 1984, Špidlík became an adviser to the Congregation for the Oriental Churches, a role in which he often quoted the words of Pope John Paul II that "the Church must breathe with both her lungs." The Pope had in fact borrowed these words from the Russian poet Vyacheslav Ivanov, and it was the legacy of the Czechs' spiritual history as a bridge between these "two lungs" which provided the inspiration for this famous motto for the dialogue between the Christian East and West:

> The phrase took wings on Saint Wenceslas' Day (according to the Byzantine calendar), 1926, when the Russian poet and thinker Vyacheslav Ivanov used it on a very special occasion. At the altar of our national saint at Saint Peter's in Rome, he made his profession of faith and pledged his allegiance to the universal Catholic Church. Soon afterwards, he wrote a poem in honour of Saint Wenceslas which begins with the words, "The light of two churches . . ." For he is a saint venerated in both East and West. In this sense, Ivanov, too, desired to be a Christian to whom both traditions were held dear.[57]

Špidlík lived out his "spirituality of unity" in the spirit of the ecumenical writings and activities of Solovyev and Ivanov. He wrote

---

57) Tomáš Špidlík, "Dýchat oběma stranami plic" [Breathing with both lungs], *Nový život* 7–8 (2001): 83.

about Solovyev's prophetic vision of the unity of the universal Church, and the search for unity among the Christians of Europe. He was keenly aware of the need for deeper theological reflection on ecumenism, about which his own views on ecclesiology were in harmony with the post-Conciliar teaching of the Catholic Church:

> Here, now, in our time, the true Church is already one. The Second Vatican Council's Decree on Ecumenism (*Unitatis redintegratio*) recognises, however, the varying degrees to which people are truly part of that Church. For the Holy Spirit fills people slowly, gradually, and those who accept the Spirit therefore unite slowly and gradually with the Church. But the fullness of the Church will be possible only at the end of time when Christ will be in everyone and everything. Ecumenism seeks these degrees of unity that it may strengthen and multiply them according to the designs of Providence and so that they may reach its fullness. Only when Catholics realise this dynamic of growth for themselves will they understand the degree to which it can be applied to others.[58]

Špidlík believes that ecumenism can be realised only through personal encounters in which the Holy Spirit is at work, making it possible for one to appreciate the spiritual gifts of the other and to offer one's own in return. For Špidlík, this meant establishing spiritual friendships, the model for which is the relationships within the Holy Trinity. Such relationships should therefore be faithful and unbreakable; they require joyful sacrifice, "because this is how the sense of unity grows and is strengthened."[59]

Špidlík often recalled the friendly reception he received in Russia and Romania:

> I once met someone who desperately wanted to know how I was received by the Orthodox in Romania. I responded drily, "I don't go to visit 'the Orthodox,' only my friends, whether Catholic or Orthodox, and my friends always receive me warmly. I have many friends there." And when in Moscow Patriarch Alexy II presented me with a gold medal and thanked me for my writing, I considered this too an expression of friendship.[60]

58) Soul of a pilgrim, 114.
59) We in the Trinity, 96.
60) Soul of a pilgrim, 115.

He was also on the receiving end of gestures of friendship from Greek Catholics and the Orthodox in Romania, such as when he was awarded an honorary doctorate from the Orthodox Theological Faculty at the University of Cluj:

> After receiving the doctorate in Cluj, I had to present a rather long lecture in a large hall. From my seat, I saw that an Orthodox metropolitan had sat down in the front row next to a Greek Catholic metropolitan. This might well have been a first. As we were at the Orthodox faculty, the sign was given to the Orthodox metropolitan to say the opening prayer, but he invited the Greek Catholic metropolitan to begin. The entire audience gratefully accepted this gesture, perhaps hardly realising or remembering that from the perspective of Church law, this had once been an impossibility.[61]

Špidlík's journey of spiritual friendship was also a journey of reconciliation between Catholic and Orthodox Christians of the Eastern Rites. But he remained a realist. He was aware that for many Orthodox the question of the role of the Greek Catholics was a contentious one, and therefore sought to deflect attention from that matter onto what he saw as the fundamentals of ecumenism:

> Even today, however, there are those who try to prove that unionism is the opposite of ecumenism. Besides, the Orthodox continue to claim that the greatest obstacle between the Catholics and the Orthodox is the Uniates. But I have an answer for that. Let us ask first, what is the essence of ecumenism after the Second Vatican Council? It is not a straightforward question of how to unite those who have been put asunder. Rather we ask, "Is our own notion of the Church so absolutely correct that it cannot include those who are divorced from us?" When we look through the old *Acta academiae velehradensis*, we find the question was often posed there. And what was said then is just as relevant today.[62]

---

61) Ibid., 117.
62) Tomáš Špidlík, "Cyrilometodějská tradice" [The Cyrillo-Methodian tradition], *Jezuité* 5 (2004): 5.

Špidlík's notion of ecumenism privileged ontological spirituality over jurisdictional considerations and saw spiritual friendship as the key bridge-builder in any dialogue between the Christian East and West. His starting point was ontological holiness, which considers holiness in terms of the manifestations of the Holy Spirit in a person's life. It is not therefore a matter of examining a person's mistakes: "After all, we are all sinners, and God loves sinners too, sometimes in a most unusual way."[63] Špidlík's focus is rather on the Holy Spirit: how the Spirit operates and is "felt"—in the language of Eastern spirituality—in the spiritual organ of the human person: in the heart that prays. In his ecumenical endeavours, Špidlík was therefore anxious to observe the manifestations of the Holy Spirit in the saints of both the Latin and the Byzantine churches. What he found was a great similarity in those manifestations, a similarity which transcended denominational boundaries. His lecture on ontological holiness in the lives of the Russian priest Saint John of Kronstadt and the Capuchin friar Saint Pio of Pietrelcina emphasised the similarity in the Spirit's gifts in these two men: spiritual guidance, discernment of a person's heart, tearful penitence over sins, continuous prayer, devotion to service through the liturgy, and veneration of the Mother of God.[64]

For Špidlík, ecumenism was not merely an academic discipline but first and foremost an encounter with a living friend in whom the Holy Spirit was at work:

> Ecumenical pronouncements are useful for the propagation of this idea, but in my experience, ecumenism is effective only through personal contact, because a human being is unrepeatable. It needs to be less of a programme and more of a mentality. When we encounter any spiritual expression we should ask, "What is good here, what is true, what can I learn?"[65]

63) Tomáš Špidlík, "Východní spiritualita" [Eastern spirituality], *Hlas Velehradu* 5 (1993): 9.
64) Tomáš Špidlík, "La carità degli stazcy: Padre Pio da Pietrelcina e Ioann di Kronštadt" [The love of the starets: Father Pio of Pietrelcina and Saint John of Kronstadt], in *Santità e carità tra Oriente e Occidente* [Love and holiness between East and West], ed. Marco Gnavi (Milan: Leonardo International, 2004), 115-131.
65) Soul of a pilgrim, 115.

Back to Velehrad

From 1991 until his death in 2010, Špidlík lived at the Centro Aletti in Rome alongside Father Marko Rupnik and six sisters from Slovenia. With its mission to represent the unity between Eastern and Western Christian spirituality through art and theological research, the Aletti has become an important meeting place for theologians and artists. It is also home to a prestigious art studio and the Lipa publishing house. The studio is best known for the design and creation of the newly renovated Redemptoris Mater Chapel in the Vatican.

On 21 October 2003, Špidlík was made a cardinal, receiving the honour from Pope John Paul II.

> When the Holy Father made me a cardinal, many figures in the Eastern Church welcomed the appointment, seeing it as Rome's recognition of the global relevance of both Eastern and Western spirituality.... Do you want to know what Velehrad means to me? It symbolised the legacy of the Fathers—a legacy I sought to preserve and promote.[66]

Even at an advanced age, Špidlík continued to preach and to lecture, to travel and to lead spiritual retreats, and he returned to Velehrad in 2007 to take part in the centenary Unionist congress. Three years later, in the early hours of 16 April 2010, Cardinal Tomáš Špidlík celebrated the final Eucharist of his earthly life. He died in Rome surrounded by his friends from the Centro Aletti at nine o'clock the same evening to the sound of the bells from the nearby church of Santa Maria Maggiore. He was buried in the apse behind the main altar of the basilica at Velehrad. The external decoration of the sarcophagus, which is situated behind the main altar of the Velehrad basilica, was designed at the art studio of the Centro Aletti in Rome under the leadership of Marko Rupnik.[67] Velehrad, his spiritual home, thus featured at the very beginning and the very end of his life's work.

66) Tomáš Špidlík, "Co pro mě znamená Velehrad?" [What does Velehrad mean to me?], *Velehradský zpravodaj* 15 (2004): 16.
67) Marko Rupnik, *Sarkofág otce Tomáše Špidlíka* [The Sarcophagus of Father Tomáš Špidlík] (Olomouc: Refugium Velehrad-Roma, 2011), 9–21.

When Cardinal Dziwisz proposed a toast to Špidlík on his 90th birthday, he drew special attention to the personification of wisdom which grew out of Špidlík's words and actions:

> It is no surprise to us that our birthday boy is known as a *starets*. The term speaks of respect and admiration for his lifelong mission and how he relates to other people. Who can count all those who have benefitted from, and continue to benefit from, his spiritual wisdom? . . . Through all the days of his long life he attained "the wisdom of the heart" (Ps 90:12). If only we could learn from him, for many years to come, how to "count our days" that we may attain at least some of that same wisdom.[68]

Understanding the significance of wisdom in Christian tradition was an important dimension of Špidlík's spirituality. Growing in wisdom was a particular feature of Slavic spirituality, so it is no surprise that the chapter on virtues in *Prameny světla* (Sources of light), the basic manual on spirituality which Špidlík wrote especially for the Czech context, opens with a discourse on wisdom. The section begins with one of Špidlík's favourite stories from the life of Saint Cyril: in a dream, Cyril is asked to choose a wife from among the girls of his town, and he chooses Sophia—Wisdom. Cyril's life of devotion to Wisdom was clearly an inspiration to Špidlík, for whom a similar devotion—a metaphorical engagement with personified Wisdom as the sought-for ideal—became an integral part of his spirituality.[69]

For Špidlík, then, wisdom is a virtue. Ancient Greek and Old Testament notions of wisdom had emphasised its practical aspects, such as craftsmanship and skilled manual work. The later Greeks would identify wisdom with the contemplation of eternal truths and the capacity for abstract thought. This was the wisdom that early and largely uneducated Christians superseded with "the wisdom of the Cross." Christian authors such as Basil the Great sought a wisdom "in which we might discover an uncontrollable urge to capture the rhythm of the cosmos, listening out for everything which grows

---

68) Stanisław Dziwisz, "Moudrost srdce" [Wisdom of the heart], in *Velehrad-Řím. Modlil se tváří k východu* [Velehrad-Rome: Praying facing East], ed. Pavel Ambros and Luisa Karczubová (Olomouc: Refugium, 2010), 13.
69) Sources of light, 175–176.

in plants, which moves in animals, which foams in the sea, and which calls out in our consciousness with an irrepressible cry, and in which we hear in a thousand words the single word 'Logos-Sophia', the Wisdom of God."[70] In Old Testament meditations, most notably in the Proverbs, wisdom was associated with the act of creation (see Prov 8:22–31), but this cosmic dimension can only be understood alongside a proper grasp of anthropology and human spirituality.

Early Christians dedicated many of their cathedrals and churches to the Wisdom of God, and Špidlík wrote about those he visited in Thessalonica and Constantinople: "Hagia Sophia is an icon of the whole world and the light of God is truly present there. Here, therefore, Wisdom is identified with the light which illuminates the whole of the cosmos."[71] Saint Cyril brought another, Slavic dimension to this approach to wisdom when he "stopped depicting divine wisdom only as a new light and began to attribute to it the form of a living person."[72]

Cyril was very much a child of Byzantine spiritual culture, and, aware of these roots, Špidlík made a detailed study of the patristic sources of Byzantine theology. For Špidlík, to become a person of great wisdom, an "author of wise words," was to become the image of God.[73] Purification from the deception, confusion, lies and illusions that stem from the Fall occurs through illumination of the intellect. Through this opening of our eyes, we once again intuitively see the truth: "[The illumined person] speaks wisely, utters knowing words and carries out their vocation to speak. . . . For we are the image of the most Holy Trinity in which the Father continuously speaks the divine *logos*. At the same time we continue in the work of the Creator through which He brings the cosmos into existence."[74] To promise oneself to wisdom is to promise oneself to eternity, to enter a living relationship with the Holy Trinity and participate in the work of creation until its completion, when God will be "all in all."

70) Ibid., 177–178.

71) Cyril and Methodius: Saints for today, 89.

72) Ibid., 90.

73) Tomáš Špidlík, "Sofiologie sv. Basila" [The sophiology of Saint Basil], in Tomáš Špidlík et al., *Od Sofie k New Age* [From Sophia to the New Age] (Olomouc: Refugium, 2001), 18.

74) Ibid.

Like Basil the Great, Špidlík was keen to explore the relationship between the wisdom of the Gospel and non-Christian, Hellenic wisdom, the wisdom from which Paul distances himself in his first letter to the Corinthians that he may follow "Christ crucified" (1 Cor 1:22). Once a diligent and first-rate scholar of Greek wisdom, Basil gradually shifted in his approach to Hellenic wisdom. After his radical conversion to the Gospel, he rejected Hellenic wisdom as foolishness and sought a true synthesis of the wisdom of natural science and Biblical revelation. He wanted to examine the visible world, to know and admire its order, but went beyond the visible and the natural when he discovered that the free act of a personal creator God lay behind the harmony of natural laws. In Basil, therefore, and also in Gregory of Nazianzus, we see some of the fundamental themes of Špidlík's theological research: the question of the existence of created and uncreated wisdom and the relationship between them; the freedom, independence and lack of determinism in a person's spiritual development and growth in wisdom; the creative co-operation—synergy—in the work of creation through wisdom that is both spoken and personified; attaining "the wisdom of the heart" in which all the antinomies of life are brought into harmony through spiritual discernment; and truly seeing and understanding the "wisdom of the Cross."

Drawing on Basil and Gregory, Špidlík emphasises the need for contemplation in the attainment of both religious and scientific knowledge. Central to Basil's journey from Hellenic to Christian wisdom was the practice of natural contemplation (*physike theoria*), in which the *logos*, the creative word of God, "speaks" through creation: "The creative word of God is 'concretised' that it may become reality, and the content of this reality is the wisdom of the world—*logos* becomes *sophia*."[75] For such wisdom to be understood, it must be spoken, expressed through a word, and must connect with human wisdom through an encounter between *sophia tou kosmou* and *anthropine sophia*.[76] We mature to this wisdom through an encounter with the spiritual and material worlds within our person:

75) Ibid., 16.
76) Ibid., 17.

Gregory of Nazianzus suggests that we are a "miraculous mixture," both spiritual and material. Only the unpredictable wisdom of God could have put together in a single person two such different worlds, and all with the special goal of sanctifying the material world. The Spirit of God sanctifies the human soul, the soul then the body, and all that is visible.[77]

The conflict between spirit and matter is a consequence of sin, but wisdom brings everything into cosmic harmony and all-unity—brings mystical insight into the "beauty" of the visible world as intended at the very moment of creation and exactly as revealed by Biblical wisdom. What is required, however, if the wisdom of the paradisiacal state is to be revealed in the image of God in which human beings were created, is purification and an ascetic struggle. Since the Incarnation, the divine-human likeness of Christ has been the ultimate model for such a restoration:

> God's image in human beings is perfected through the virtues, and so our union with God is deepened. This union is realised through Christ, hence Origen identified the virtues with Christ.[78]

Špidlík offers much practical wisdom on how we can creatively form our inner life and reflect intelligently on our acts and intentions. Referring to Proverbs 2:6, he reminds us that Biblical wisdom is associated with knowledge and understanding, with the ability to know and correctly evaluate the meaning of events that are taking place and to direct them creatively towards a desired goal. He also mentions the paradox of "the wisdom of the Cross," and suggests that Christians "are able to make use even of falls and failures. This is the 'wisdom of the Cross' that we find in Saint Paul."[79]

He also teaches us how to grow in wisdom and prudence and attain a state of *apatheia*: not to do anything recklessly or when we are angry, sad or agitated, but to think matters over properly once we have calmed down; not to allow ourselves to be influenced by bias or prejudice; when we stray into unfamiliar ground, to consult

---

77) Key to the unknown, 65.
78) Sources of light, 171.
79) In your footsteps, 106.

someone who understands such matters; to learn from our elders and from good literature; to avoid making the same mistake twice; to envisage the consequences of our actions; to ask ourselves, "What do I want to do? Why? How? Where? What is going to come out of it? Am I up to it?"[80]

Špidlík's early work was inspired by his Jesuit formation and by classical ascetic manualistics. Later, however, as a lecturer in Eastern spirituality at the Pontifical Oriental Institute, he set his advice in the wider context of theological life and the Christian worldview inspired by Russian authors such as Solovyev and Bulgakov, but also Pavel Florensky, Vasily Zenkovsky and Vladimir Ern, whose thinking he drew together with that of others in his seminal *Ruská idea* (The Russian idea). The final section of *Ruská idea* is devoted to the teaching of the Russian philosophers and theologians on personified divine Wisdom, or sophiology, a highly controversial subject even within Russian thought: "The problem of understanding [sophiology] is often posited wrongly: sophiology presupposes a spiritual vision which is difficult to harmonise with the rational terms through which we draw near to that vision."[81] The terms used in sophiology are symbols that provide initiation into a mystery which transcends them. Drawing especially on Florensky, Špidlík explores the sophiological application of wisdom to Christ, to the Mother of God, to a vision of personified cosmic "pan-unity," and to the Church. Wisdom is incarnated into the world that it may transform it, and through wisdom we are able intuitively to take possession of the truth "as something concrete expressed by a symbol."[82]

In an intuitive spiritual vision of beauty, Wisdom-Sophia "is like a radiance, and this radiance is also a vision of multiple harmonious relationships."[83] Špidlík frames this mystical notion of wisdom within the teaching of Eastern Christianity on "uncreated energies." In such a vision, God enters the world through uncreated Sophia, who transforms the world. Her most complete personification in the economy of salvation is Jesus Christ, who unlike Sophia is "the fullness of the Godhead" (Col 2:9 KJV). Špidlík is very clear that "divine

80) Ibid., 106–107.
81) Russian idea, 316.
82) Ibid., 319.
83) Ibid., 324.

Sophia denotes God only insofar as God reveals himself externally; it is thus not the fullness of God."[84] The distinction is analogous to that between the essence and energies of God, as described by Gregory Palamas and later by Sergei Bulgakov:

> Would it not be possible to see in the same connection two Sophias: a created Sophia and an uncreated Sophia? Through these two, God reveals himself and is perceived as revealed. Palamas thought of the divine energies as the revelation of God's essence; Bulgakov also uses the word Sophia for God's essence as revealed first in God and subsequently in creation. She is not God but the content of God's ideas, the words of the Word, and the life of the Holy Spirit.[85]

It becomes clear that in Špidlík's thinking, wisdom is neither the fullness of God nor simply something "created." Wisdom has two faces: she reveals herself as uncreated in the form of the divine creative love of God, and as created and emanating from creation according to its level of "sophianity." Any other expressions and terms concerning wisdom are "not the fruit of the metaphysical reflections of certain thinkers but rather an expression of a mystical experience that reveals to us in a particular divine vision how everything created permeates the uncreated life of God in the Trinity."[86]

Having explored the cosmic, anthropological and mystical notions of wisdom in Špidlík's writing, we will conclude our reflections on the "wisdom of the Cross" with a brief consideration of the Marian dimension. To explore and explain this theme, Špidlík uses the Biblical story of Jacob's return to Palestine (Gen 32–33) and the warm welcome he receives from Esau, not because of his riches but paradoxically because of the pitiful state he was in after his struggle with the "mysterious man":

> It was not Jacob's power and strength which impressed his brother but rather his wretched state, his weakness. This explains very clearly the mystery of the Cross: victory and success are gained through failure.

---

84) Ibid., 326.
85) Ibid., 327.
86) Ibid., 338.

Those who read the Scriptures with understanding will discover just how often this motif is repeated there.[87]

So this wisdom, which is foolishness to the world, is truly a paradox: weakness, suffering, failing and falling are what bring success and ultimate victory.

Drawing on the Ignatian exercises, Špidlík offers us two images: one of Mary, Mother of Sorrows, looking with sadness upon her newborn child and to all that lay ahead of him; and the other of the Pietà, where beneath the cross, Christ's mother cradles the body of her dead son. Špidlík suggests that it was Jesus himself who resolved Mary's doubts about the meaning of life:

> In drawing his life as a teacher to a close, Christ leaves his most beautiful lesson for the perfect disciple, his mother: he teaches her the wisdom of the Cross, explains the deep meaning of life, which in the eyes of others has nothing but a tragic, senseless end. The Mother of God stretches her hand towards him in a gesture that says "I accept."[88]

At that moment, we truly see the wisdom of the Cross: wisdom which turns suffering into salvation.

> In his hour of death, Jesus thirsts for everything that is realised before God to be realised completely, cosmically. This thirst is to be inherited by all who believe in him. As soon as they feel this thirst, they receive the gift of the Holy Spirit, the living water that will transform the desert of their lives into a paradise.[89]

Such indeed is the wisdom of the Cross.

87) Ibid., 117.
88) I was born for higher things, 326.
89) Ibid., 339.

A SYNTHESIS OF THE SPIRITUAL THEOLOGY
OF THE CHRISTIAN EAST AND WEST

As a teacher of spiritual theology with a particular expertise in patristics and Russian thought, Špidlík made a lifelong study of the spiritual life, which he explored, analysed and presented as part of a complex and overarching Christian worldview. In this section, we will explore two of the more significant aspects of Špidlík's thinking: the Holy Spirit and its role in the spiritual life, and the Eucharist as a source of spiritual vitality. We will conclude by examining the influence of the *Philokalia* on Špidlík's spiritual theology.

THE HOLY SPIRIT AND THE SPIRITUAL LIFE

Špidlík explored the term "spiritual" in some depth in *The Spirituality of the Christian East*, beginning with the philosophers and spiritual writers and their views on the notion of the spirit. He was anxious to defend the personal nature of the Holy Spirit and its relation to the two divine persons who had been the dominant dogmatic subjects of the early Councils.

> The decisive characteristic of the concept of spirit in Scripture, as distinct from that found in philosophic reflection, lies in its immediate association with the person of God (and not as the more or less divine element in the human person). The spirit of God in action is manifested in increasing measure through the history of salvation; in Saint Paul it becomes the foundation of the Christian life: "the spirit of God," "the spirit of Christ," "the spirit of the Lord," and the Holy Spirit. . . . The human person is qualified as *pneumatikos* (spiritual) through the operation of the Spirit (*apo tēs tou Pneumatos energeias*).[90]

The Holy Spirit's role in the spiritual life is completely central for Špidlík. The spiritual life is lived "in the Spirit and with the Holy Spirit,"[91] and its goal is perfection in every aspect of human nature:

---

90) *Systematic Handbook*, 29-30.
91) Sources of light, 13.

In the perfect human being, all aspects of the personality are united, all are permeated with the vivifying power of the Holy Spirit. It is thus rightly said that the goal of the spiritual life is the perfect spiritualisation of the whole person: mind, will, feelings and body.[92]

An ascent to God in the Holy Spirit is complemented by the descent of God into the human heart so that God's life, the life of the Holy Trinity, may be revealed in that person: "If the spiritual life is the presence and activity of the Holy Spirit in us, then we can also say that it is the life of God, the divine life, in the human person."[93] In *Prayer*, volume two of *The Spirituality of the Christian East*, Špidlík expresses the Trinitarian dimension of the spiritual life as a dialogical synergy between these ascending and descending movements:

When Christ revealed the identity of the Father and of God, he set this revelation within another mystery, which the traditional formulations epitomise by two movements: one descending—every good comes to us from the Father, through the Son, in the Holy Spirit; the other, ascending—we ascend to the Father, through the Son, in the Holy Spirit.[94]

With this twofold spiritual movement in mind, we may, with Špidlík, want to ask two fundamental questions regarding the role of the Holy Spirit in the spiritual life: 1. Is the presence of the Holy Spirit, who is distinct from creation, only an external agent in a person's sanctification? And related to this, what is the relationship between the Holy Spirit and the soul, and the Holy Spirit and the body, and how is the experience of the Holy Spirit manifested? 2. Is salvation through the person of the Holy Spirit achieved solely through the activity of the Spirit, or in harmony with the other two divine persons?

---

92) Ibid., 32.
93) Ibid., 17.
94) Tomáš Špidlík, *Prayer*, trans. Anthony Gythiel (Kalamazoo, MI: Cistercian Publications, 2005), 38 (original title: *La spiritualité de l'Orient chrétien II. La prière.*)

The Ascending Dimension of Spiritual-Physical Life in the Holy Spirit

Špidlík always considered the human person as a whole, as a unity, the spiritual and physical dimensions as a single entity. The activity of the Holy Spirit thus affects the whole person. The effect is internal and results from the indwelling of the Spirit; evil spirits, by contrast, affect a person only from the outside. Špidlík follows Irenaeus in calling the Holy Spirit the "soul of our soul."[95] The Holy Spirit spiritualises the soul and the body, bringing them gradually into harmony:

> If we are concerned to fulfil all the Holy Spirit asks of us, then He himself will teach us how to harmonise his demands with the demands of other parts of the person. In other words, the needs of the soul and the body will no longer be in conflict.[96]

The tension between the needs of the soul and the needs of the body is thus tempered, and the body itself participates in the inner transformation the Holy Spirit brings. Špidlík rehabilitates physicality by suggesting that it is predestined—that is, predisposed—to spiritualisation. He is aware that in the Pauline New Testament "the body" is synonymous with sinful desires that act against the operation of the Holy Spirit. But while such egoism is manifested through the body, the body must nonetheless participate in a person's gradual spiritualisation. There is no place here for a radical dualism of body and soul: physical and spiritual life are one. Feelings can reflect what is taking place on the spiritual-physical level but here, too, we must be cautious. The Messalians—Euchites—incorrectly identified feelings of pleasure or displeasure with the presence or absence of grace in the spiritual life. Špidlík admits that our emotions play a significant role in identifying the inner workings of the Holy Spirit, but warns against an unhealthy fixation on them because the dangers of illusion, false emotions and mental illness are ever present. His exploration of spiritual feelings did lead him to regard "emotional" knowledge of the operation of the Holy Spirit as a sign of the

95) Do you know God the Father? 128–129.
96) Ibid., 130.

quickening of the soul and of an awareness of the sweetness of God's presence: "Although spiritual feelings are not the only manifestation of the divine life in a Christian soul, they are nonetheless a sign of spiritual health."[97] But he also suggested that "the level of deification cannot be identified with a conscious experience of the presence of the Spirit."[98] Indeed, the Holy Spirit transforms a person's affective life, liberating it from "animalistic feelings":

> We perceive bodily feelings as the lowest and crudest, "like those of an animal." Their untamed nature, which disturbs human unity, is the consequence of sin. They are stilled by the operation of the Spirit and become useful to the spiritual person. The perfect ones thus reach a state in which they "feel God" even in their own body.[99]

So, although as human beings we have the capacity to experience the Holy Spirit through our feelings, their very fragility and the permanent threat of self-delusion mean they cannot be made the principal criteria for judging the authenticity of an ascent to God; the temptation to excessive self-reflection is only too clear. An experience of the Holy Spirit always carries an inner tension: with spiritual union comes the realisation of one's weakness and ignorance, which in turn creates the awareness of a great chasm. A person through whom the Holy Spirit is working thus never fully identifies their own person with the Holy Spirit but is aware of being both graced and at the same time inadequate.

Other signs of the presence of the Holy Spirit include love of and martyrdom for Christ, and "a pure faith, a good life, the virtues, and uncorrupted morals."[100] Špidlík explains the different workings of the Holy Spirit by reference to the various names the Spirit is given: Life-giver of the soul; Enlightener through the true light of Christ; Purifier, forgiver of sins, giver of tears to those who repent, and teacher of all the virtues.[101]

97) *Systematic Handbook*, 72–73.
98) Tomáš Špidlík, *Vnitřně zakoušet. Eseje pro duchovní život* [Inner experience: Essays on the spiritual life] (Olomouc: Refugium Velehrad-Roma, 2009), 183.
99) Russian idea, 274.
100) Sources of light, 34.
101) *Systematic Handbook*, 32–33.

Inner transformation through the Holy Spirit is not purely a human concern. Špidlík always emphasised the reciprocal connection between the human and cosmic dimensions of the spiritual life and the gradual spiritualisation of the whole of humanity and of the cosmos:

> The spiritual life has . . . a decisive effect upon our relationship with our neighbour and also with non-rational nature, the whole cosmic order. Placed in the visible world, human beings achieve their spiritual goal through "cosmic spiritualisation."[102]

> The entire cosmos is regenerated by the Holy Spirit and thus forms a single temple. The journey to this ideal is a long one, both in the history of the world and in the life of an individual.[103]

The special calling of human beings, then, is to spiritualise not just everything around them but also human history and the whole of the cosmos.

The Descending, Revelatory Dimension of Spiritual Life in the Holy Trinity

In exploring an ascent to God through the work of the Holy Spirit, which is manifested by the inner transformation of our spiritual-physical faculties and the spiritualisation of the whole cosmos, we answered our first question: Is the presence of the Holy Spirit only an external agent in our sanctification?

A consideration of the opposite movement, the descending dimension of spirituality, an encounter with the revelation of the life of the divine Trinity into which we who are transformed by the activity of the Holy Spirit are drawn, will lead us to our second question: Is salvation through the Holy Spirit an activity of the Spirit alone, or is it performed in co-operation with the other two divine persons? Christian orthodoxy insists on the latter, that salvation in the Holy Spirit and the transformation that comes with it takes place in synergy and harmony with the Father and the Son: "The activity of

---

102) Ibid., 33.
103) Do you know God the Father? 130.

the Holy Spirit who is present within us enables us to communicate in a real and living way with Jesus and the Father; it deifies us."[104]

The Trinitarian dimension of the spiritual life was key for Špidlík and a subject much under discussion at the time he was writing and making his insightful contributions. Špidlík expounded on how the spiritual life is permeated with the divine life, and emphasised the importance of both an experience of and an inner adherence to the doctrine of the Holy Trinity.

> Mystics express the same mystery in two different ways: either the Most Holy Trinity descends among us, into our world; or we and our world are drawn from below, upwards, into the heart of the life of God.[105]

Through Trinitarian sanctification we become the dwelling place of the Holy Spirit through the redemptive work of Jesus Christ so that God the Father becomes our Father:[106]

> In the Spirit, through the Son, human beings are led to the Father, into Trinitarian life, into that inner life, into the eternal dialogue of the Trinity. The experience of mystics from both East and West attests to this.[107]

Špidlík often explored the revelation of the Holy Trinity through the experience of the great mystics. Many Western Christian mystics—Hildegard of Bingen, Gertrude the Great, Jan van Ruysbroeck, Catherine of Siena, Teresa of Avila, John of the Cross, Ignatius of Loyola, Elisabeth of the Trinity—testify to an inner revelation, to an intimate encounter with the mystery of the Holy Trinity. They speak of entering into the silence of the Trinity, into an experience of eternity, of rest, peace and tranquillity and the fullness of life and love, in contrast to the unrest and disorder of the world.[108] In a descending "chain of holiness," Špidlík commences with the holiness of the self-revealing Trinity and its anchoring in the sacramental life of the Church; he then descends, "lower," to the Trinitarian features

---

104) Inner experience, 181.
105) Do you know God the Father? 132.
106) Ibid., 132–133.
107) Russian idea, 53.
108) We in the Trinity, 17–22.

of particular Christian states—priesthood, marriage, monasticism—and of human relationships and the moral life. The Second Vatican Council spoke of marriage as a "domestic church"; as a reflection of the Holy Trinity. A life of chastity is defensible only if it is considered a spiritual marriage and an anticipation of the angelic state in the love of the Holy Trinity. Friendships, too, like the relationships within the Trinity, are to be faithful, reciprocal and indissoluble. Finally, for each individual, the journey to Trinitarian perfection concerns coming to know who I am, who you are, who he or she is, and being led into truth and complete freedom in relationships of love:

> The mystery of the most Holy Trinity is the key to understanding the reality of the world. It is a dialogue with the author of things, a personal conversation that is not poetic licence or a childish illusion. Indeed it is not even abstract impersonal knowledge, but an experience of mutual love.[109]

Seen from below, the spiritual life is an ascending journey of transformation by the Holy Spirit through which the believer is led into a state of deification by the revelation of the life of the Holy Trinity, thus acquiring, in the Holy Spirit, new knowledge and new wisdom. This transformation encompasses the whole of the believer's life and all their relationships, which come to reflect the life of the Holy Trinity. Seen from above, it is through the descent and activity of the divine persons that believers find wisdom for the choices they make in fulfilling their calling.

> The personal indwelling of the Spirit in the soul is a participation in the life of the Holy Trinity. While considering this mystery of union, we are also justified in insisting on the distinction between persons. The soul does not lose herself in some nirvana; on the contrary, she maintains her personality and develops it to the highest degree, even if, for the moment and in full freedom, she has sacrificed the use of her human faculties.[110]

---

109) Ibid., 110.
110) *Prayer*, 228.

Although mystical ecstasy bears elements of passive acceptance and the abandonment of our physical faculties, every such inpouring is accompanied by a co-operation, a synergy, between the human will and the will of God, between the human will and grace.[111] This active co-operation with grace is a "theurgic" co-operation, although it can sometimes manifest itself in what may appear to be external passivity and resignation, like death on a cross. The ascetic inner life always entails co-operation, and the search for this co-operation entails a lifelong inner dialogue, a life of prayer, where the ascending and descending dimensions of the spiritual life meet, and where each acquires its own dynamic of growth towards perfection.

The Dialogical Dimension of Life in the Holy Spirit

Prayer is the only way to develop spiritually and to experience the working of the Holy Spirit in the spiritual life, which is why Špidlík's output on the subject was so considerable.

> The nearness between our spirit and God is established above all in prayer, which is uttered "in Spirit." According to the beautiful expression of Theophan the Recluse, prayer is "the breathing of the Spirit." Speaking to God presupposes some form of inspiration, since the human person in prayer is "under the guidance of the Spirit of God."[112]

If the Holy Spirit is the "soul of our soul," transforming our spiritual-physical life and enabling us to enter the life of God and receive the revelation of the Holy Trinity, it is the "breathing of the Spirit" which provides the inner dynamic for such an encounter: only in prayer do we experience the mystery of an encounter with the persons of the Holy Trinity.

> Without the Spirit, prayer would not be Christological. For Saint Paul, being "in Christ Jesus" (Rom 8:1) means living by "the Spirit" (Rom 8:2). The Paraclete is "the Spirit of adoption," in whom we cry, "*Abba*, Father" (Rom 8:15; Gal 4:6). The Spirit lets us repeat the gestures of Christ, because he is the Spirit of Jesus. He prolongs the thanksgiving of Jesus

111) Sources of light, 60–61.
112) *Prayer*, 39.

in the breaking of the bread, and enables us to repeat the prayer of Jesus.[113]

As it was for the Eastern Christian authors, so for Špidlík prayer is a kind of "natural breathing," a return to the lost paradisiacal nature of the image of God. This image is restored by attaining the divine likeness as incarnated in the divine-human nature of Jesus Christ.

> [Prayer] should be like the natural breathing of the heart which longs for union with God spontaneously and through a natural intuition senses the presence of the Holy Spirit in everything the human person does, thinks, and desires. Such prayer is unceasing. It is, to the extent to which it is possible to feel and taste the presence of the Spirit in this life, an awareness of our state as children of God, of our deification.[114]

Every prayer is therefore an *epiclesis*, a plea for the presence of the Holy Spirit, as "human words ascend to, penetrate into, so to speak, the inner conversation between the Father and the Son only through the power of the Holy Spirit."[115] The Holy Spirit and the prayers of the spiritual life are mutually entwined, and this relationship reaches its height in the celebration of the Eucharist:

> The personal nature of the intimacy between our spirit and God means that it is dialogic and finds its ultimate expression in prayer. This is why we pray in the Spirit. In that sense, every prayer contains an implicit *epiclesis* so that the prayer itself is uttered in the power of the Holy Spirit because it is an "elevation of the Spirit" (with a capital "S"). And indeed, in the Eucharistic prayer, *epiclesis* is explicitly present.[116]

Špidlík reminds us that "in the Latin rite, this [*epiclesis*] is expressed by the invocation of the Holy Spirit at the beginning of every significant liturgical function: 'Come, Holy Spirit!'"[117] Christian

113) Ibid.
114) Ibid., 258-259.
115) Sources of light, 406.
116) Inner experience, 180.
117) Sources of light, 406.

spiritual life, life in the Holy Spirit, is therefore rooted in Eucharistic spirituality.

Špidlík was not only a spiritual theologian, he was also a priest for whom the centre of the spiritual life was the celebration of the Eucharist, through which the believer enters fully into the mystery of the life of the Holy Trinity.

Here, we will follow the Eucharistic liturgy from *epiclesis*, through *anamnesis*, to the receiving of the elements. The invocation of the Holy Spirit (*epiclesis*) is a plea for the transformation of the elements and of the communicants through the work of all three persons of the Holy Trinity. The remembrance (*anamnesis*) of the institution of the Eucharist through the very words of Jesus Christ is metaphysical: it makes the past a present reality, and deepens the significance of memory in Christian spirituality. Receiving the Eucharist deepens spiritual life itself.

Transformation in the Holy Spirit:
Epiclesis and the Deification of Humanity

Epiclesis is a humble request which through the intercession of Christ becomes a certainty. Liturgists and theologians use the term *epiclesis* for the prayer which asks, which entreats, over the bread and wine, for the "intervention" of the Holy Spirit to transform the elements into the body and blood of Jesus Christ, and which makes the same urgent plea for the transformation of the communicants. A mass structured in this manner emphasises a theological principle: the Eucharistic prayer is Trinitarian. The consecration is therefore attributed to three divine persons: the Father, insofar as it represents an act of divine power; the priesthood of the Son, which renews the mystery of the Last Supper on the altar; finally, this mystery is the special work of the Holy Spirit, to whom we attribute the work of sanctification.[118]

118) Tomáš Špidlík, *Eucharistie. Lék nesmrtelnosti* [The Eucharist: Medicine of immortality] (Olomouc: Refugium Velehrad-Roma, 2005), 44.

The spiritual life of a Christian disciple is founded on an experience of divine revelation, and it is clear from Špidlík's teaching that during the liturgical *epiclesis* this revelation is Trinitarian. The *epiclesis* therefore provides a model for the person who is seeking, through prayer, to enter the communion of loving relationships in the Holy Trinity. And because *epiclesis* also includes a prayer for the inner transformation of the communicants, this transformation, the sanctification of the whole of a believer's spiritual life, is also Trinitarian.

As we have already suggested, two movements are taking place during the celebration of the Eucharist: a descent and an ascent. During the invocation, the Trinity descends, and we are drawn up into the very heart of God; this encounter takes place through prayer, dialogically. Prayer in the Holy Spirit supplies the energy for the very transformation for which we are praying: "Through prayer, the body itself is on its way to 'spiritualisation' and to recovering its proper nature."[119]

Here Špidlík is referring to the theological anthropology of the Eastern Church with its emphasis on "deification," a process by which the human person returns to the lost paradisiacal nature through being likened to the divine-human nature of Jesus Christ. God's life in human beings, the dynamic process of deification, is the working of the Holy Spirit within us,[120] and the *epiclesis* reminds us of this divine activity. This transformation by the Holy Spirit affects us in our very essence, ontologically, transforming human nature so that it may participate in divine nature. During the invocation of the Holy Spirit and the prayer for the transformation of the bread and wine into the body and blood of Christ, human nature is transformed, deified by the Holy Spirit: "Although possessing the Spirit, the Church invokes him in the *epiclesis*, so that he may descend not only on the Eucharistic 'gifts,' but also 'upon us.'"[121] Whenever we pray, we present ourselves in the same way that we present the elements, as a sacrifice: "Every prayer uttered in the Spirit contains an implied *epiclesis*."[122]

119) *Prayer*, 76.
120) Sources of light, 18.
121) *Prayer*, 108.
122) Ibid., 40.

Like spiritual life in general, the celebration of the Eucharist is experienced in dynamic-eschatological anticipation: we are being transformed here and now but we also anticipate the eschatological fulfilment that we will not attain during our earthly lives. The invocation during the *epiclesis* thus provides a foretaste of the full outpouring of the Holy Spirit at the end of the ages. Those who are already being transformed and purified by the Holy Spirit experience the fruits of a life lived in holiness, but a holiness that will reach perfection only in eternity. Purification and moments of inner illumination lead to gradual unification with the Triune God, a unification that is experienced sacramentally, within a church community, and is therefore ecclesiastical in nature:

> A full outpouring of the Spirit is promised at the end of time, at the eschatological completion. But we are already, now, able to participate in it through the Eucharistic prayer, which unfolds in time but essentially transcends time. That the saints would "lose all sense of time" while praying is not merely a psychological phenomenon of the power of concentration: it is truly a crossing over to eternity. The Eucharistic prayer takes place "through Christ, with Christ and in Christ." Jesus' time is not simply of earthly duration, since he lives and reigns forever with the Father and the Holy Spirit. Spiritualised by the Spirit, his Eucharistic body will become heavenly, the bread of angels, and at the same time the bread of pilgrims on their way to eternity (*panis angelorum factum cibus viatorum*).[123]

Remembrance in the Mystery of the Eucharist: *Anamnesis* as a Door to Divine Memory

> *Anamnesis* is a memorial, a remembrance. The great Orthodox theologian and liturgist Alexander Schmemann calls the Eucharist "a sacrament of remembrance." As an expression of obedience to the Lord's command, "do this in remembrance of me," the celebration of the Eucharist is therefore defined as a "remembrance."[124]

123) Tomáš Špidlík, "Nell'Eucaristia lo Spirito Santo illumina, purifica e unifica" [The work of the Holy Spirit in the Eucharist: Illumination, purification and unification], in *Potenza divina d'amore* [The divine power of love] 14, no. 5 (2005): no page numbers.
124) The Eucharist, 12.

Remembrance opens up the memory of a past event and in so doing makes that event present not only in the imagination but also, through its effects, in reality. An historical revelation of God is brought into the present by the proclamation of the Word, drawing us into the events of the history of salvation. Listening to the words of Christ is one of the most basic spiritual activities for a Christian. Christ's words expose us to the same energy that healed, forgave and encouraged faith during Jesus' earthly ministry, and affirm now, as they did then, his messianic calling. Through the Eucharistic prayer, when the priest proclaims the words Jesus used at the institution of the Eucharist, liturgical space and time become metaphysically connected with the eternal heavenly liturgy:

> The Eucharist unites souls and events across time and space. It is a memorial not merely to the past but also of the time to come when Christ will appear in glory. The prayers given the name *anamnesis* (remembrance) thus summarise what is, according to the Syriac term used to designate them, *mdabranoûto* (economy), the entire economy of Christ . . .[125]

In Christian spirituality, seeing plays as important a role as hearing, and Špidlík explored the influence of art on spirituality, and vice versa, on numerous occasions. The liturgical space where the word is proclaimed is also a place where art is employed to mediate, symbolically, the meeting of temporality and eternity during the liturgical act. In Eastern Christianity, liturgical *anamnesis* is represented visually by the iconostasis:

> An indispensable element in Russian churches, the iconostasis is an expression of the ecclesiastical liturgical *anamnesis*. It both conceals the mysterious ministrations of the priest and reveals them through a visible representation of what takes place invisibly in the Eucharist. Liturgical *anamnesis* is a remembrance of Christ and the whole history of salvation. The image of the Pantocrator surrounded by the heavenly powers and the saints (the Virgin, John the Baptist, and the apostles) thus establishes the "order" of the iconostasis.[126]

125) Ibid., 118.
126) Russian idea, 311.

Aural and visual perceptions spark the imagination, the inner world, in which the human memory with all its recollections also plays a part. When the human, psychological memory meets the memory of God, it acquires a metaphysical dimension in which the believer enters the story of salvation as played out through the life of the pilgrim church. Because temporality and eternity are united in the resurrected Christ, our commemoration of the mystery of Christ's divine-human life makes the historical event of the Last Supper a present reality:[127]

> When we celebrate the Eucharist, the space and time of the people gathered together "expands"; we become contemporaries of the suffering of the Lord. . . . The cross and resurrection of Jesus present the possibility of a new existence, of every person opening up to God and to others, so realising the goal of communion with the Father.[128]

What is remembered liturgically becomes a present reality: *anamnesis* draws in our individual memories, purifies our memory as a whole, and brings God's acts of salvation into our lives in the here and now. We recognise this process from our everyday lives, such as in our fondness for photographs of our loved ones, especially those who have passed away:

> Memories play an important role in our lives. Every act of remembrance seeks to allow what happened in history to last, in a certain sense, for eternity. The person who keeps a photograph of their deceased mother is saying that she lives on in their memory, especially when they are actually looking at the photo.[129]

During such a recapitulation before God, eternal and temporal memory meet each other, and this encounter will be especially intense at the moment of death. During the liturgical celebration, our memory and personal recollections become part of the divine

127) Tomáš Špidlík, "L'Eucatistia – anamnesi dell'eternità" [The Eucharist: Anamnesis of eternity], in *Il Volto dei Volti Cristo* [The face of the faces of Christ] (Gorle: Velar, 2000), 4:8-10.
128) The Eucharist, 14.
129) Nell'Eucaristia, no page number.

memory, and one day we will enter that memory with our whole life. Špidlík was keenly aware of the relationship between the Eucharist and our entry into eternity:

> Through the Eucharist, we too, our lives, our good deeds, enter eternity, and all becomes divine-human thanks to the grace of the Spirit. The celebration of the Eucharist is an anticipation of the Heavenly liturgy in which, at the heavenly altar, Christ the eternal High Priest remembers our earthly life, and in which is celebrated an eternal remembrance of the whole history of salvation.[130]

Receiving the Eucharist: Sustenance for the Spiritual Battle and a Foretaste of Eternity

At a critical point in the Eucharist there comes a moment of death, "when we give up the bread by which we live and offer it to God on the altar."[131] In this symbolic sacrifice, we renounce the very thing that keeps us alive, the nourishment without which our physical bodies cannot exist. It is a reckoning with death: "Why do we sacrifice the elements? That we may receive them back transformed, deified. They are the symbols of our life, a life thwarted by death, but a life we regain through the resurrection."[132]

This is why the Eucharist culminates in the receiving of the body and blood of Jesus Christ. Receiving the elements strengthens our faith and hope in an immediate and intimate experience of eternal life:

> The Eucharist is the power that brings resurrection. It is the "medicine of immortality," as Ignatius of Antioch said. It enables the whole of our life and the life of the world to be permeated with the very energy of God. The bread we receive is not simply bread but the divine bread for all. The death and resurrection of Jesus Christ enabled the whole of creation to enter the glory. In the Eucharist, we are offered a new way which opens itself to all creation, the way of transformation, as we too are enabled to become one with the power of the resurrection.[133]

130) The Eucharist, 15.
131) Ibid., 29.
132) Ibid., 30.
133) Ibid., 58.

The resurrection is the cornerstone of the spiritual life. Without faith in the resurrection, our emotions, our will and our intellect would never become fully formed and we would be destined to a life of unhealthy self-centredness. Received in complete faith in the resurrection, the Eucharist has the power to free us from self-centeredness, transform us into the likeness of Christ's divinity-humanity, and lead us along the path of inner surrender towards a complete giving and sacrificing of our lives for others, by which, paradoxically, life will be returned to us in the perfect fullness of the resurrection:

> We seek to revive that way of thinking which is in harmony with the Eucharist, especially the spirit of sacrifice: "Christ will become a sacrifice for us in the full sense of the word when we become a sacrifice for him," writes Gregory the Great. In times of persecution, the churches always felt a close connection between receiving communion and martyrdom.[134]

We may enter death alone, but through the resurrection we become members of the heavenly community. Although we are not always aware of it, receiving the Eucharist strengthens our sense of communion with the martyrs, saints and angels who accompany us in our spiritual life; the Eucharist connects us to the age to come:

> Contemporary Orthodox writers like to emphasise the "doxological" character of the liturgy, which forms a unity between the *anamnesis* and the Eucharist. In receiving the Eucharist, we partake in the heavenly feast in the kingdom of God. Through the praise and vigilance which bring us into service of the "vigilant"—the angels, martyrs and saints—the soul even now becomes a part of the blessed reality of the age to come. . . . Moreover, the commemoration and proclamation of the Parousia makes the present time, a time of "purification," vibrantly alive. It is an embryonic state, although one that is controlled simultaneously by the hope of an ascent to the light and a fear of falling.[135]

134) Sources of light, 137.
135) Tomáš Špidlík, *Věřím v život věčný. Eschatologie* [I believe in eternal life: Eschatology] (Olomouc: Refugium Velehrad-Roma, 2007), 88.

Receiving the Eucharist heals and transforms us, cleanses us from temptation and sin, and unites us with Christ and with one another.[136] The Eucharist reinforces the sanctifying power of grace, protects us from venial and mortal sins and evil spirits and enables us to stand up to sinful inclinations; it strengthens our prayer life, provides nourishment for the soul and brings joy and solace in equal measure.[137] It also has a therapeutic effect on the body, which in receiving the Eucharist becomes a holy temple, like the body of the Virgin Mary at the moment of the Incarnation; the Eucharist calms our senses and emotions, protects us from danger, and provides assurance of the resurrection and of our immortality.[138]

The Eucharist also strengthens the spiritual life with regard to watchfulness and guarding the heart from egoistic thoughts and the *logismoi*, which come from outside rather than from within and are the source of the passions that lead to sin: "The art of preserving the paradise of the heart in a state of innocence lies in rejecting every insinuation of the enemy from the outset."[139] The Eucharist provides irreplaceable support in this spiritual struggle. It is the source of grace that enables discernment of our thoughts and protects us from the thoughts that would lead us from the straight path and from our true calling and vocation.

The Eucharist brings such a degree of inner transformation that the believer is able to return to their everyday life with renewed energy. It represents not just resurrection, transformation, an ascent, but also a descent into day-to-day earthly life so that every moment can be experienced liturgically—Eucharistically. We see a symbol of this divine-human transformation in the processions that take place on the feast of Corpus Christi:

Carried out into our towns and cities, the Eucharist symbolises the fact that this nourishment provides us with the strength to transform our surroundings, our lives together, the whole of society. When Cardinal Beran became Archbishop of Prague, he promoted the motto "Eucharist and work." The war had just ended and endless talks about re-building

136) The Eucharist, 65–70.
137) Sources of light, 134–135.
138) Ibid., 136.
139) Russian idea, 282.

our state had begun. The archbishop wanted to emphasise that this re-building, this work, would be blessed only if it was supported by grace. Only then would the work be joyful and effective.[140]

The relationship between *theoria* (the contemplation of love) and *praxis* (loving actions) was a regular theme of Špidlík's reflections on Christian spirituality.[141] Every human being seeks a sense of harmony between contemplation and work, and the two are intimately linked in the Eucharist. Love cannot be closed in upon itself; rather, as with the relationships within the Trinity, love will seek to give itself to the other, to work for the other. Without the Eucharist, work is a burden; with the Eucharist, work is transformed and provided with new meaning. The Eucharist transforms us, therefore, so that we in turn may transform every moment of our lives.

THE INFLUENCE OF THE *PHILOKALIA* ON ŠPIDLÍK'S SPIRITUAL THEOLOGY

The *Philokalia* is a collection of the writings of the Church Fathers deposited in the libraries of Mount Athos. The title was probably inspired by a work of the same name, an anthology of the writings of Origen by Basil the Great and Gregory of Nazianzus. There are two early editions: the first, the Greek edition, was compiled by Macarius of Corinth and Nicodemus the Hagiorite and published in Venice in 1782; the second, the *Dobrotolubiye*, is in Church Slavonic and was published in Moscow in 1793. The latter was collated independently of the former by Paisius Velichkovsky but was clearly influenced by the Greek edition and contains most of the Greek texts. Both books are the fruit of a desire to effect the spiritual renewal of the Church through a renaissance of the spirituality of the Church Fathers. The work includes "sentences" written from the time of Anthony the Great to teachers of the patristic period such as Evagrius Ponticus, John Cassian, Isaiah the Solitary, Maximus the Confessor, and other Byzantine Hesychasts such as Nikephoros the Monk, Gregory of Si-

---

140) Tomáš Špidlík, "Procesí Božího těla" [Corpus Christi processions], *Nový život* 6 (2000): 103.
141) See, for example, *Systematic Handbook*, 66.

nai, Gregory Palamas, Symeon of Thessalonica and Symeon the New Theologian. In the nineteenth century, the book was translated into Russian by Bishop Ignatius Brianchaninov and shortly afterwards by Theophan the Recluse. The main themes are inner prayer, watchfulness, and the constant remembrance of God.[142]

The *Philokalia* in Špidlík's Writings

Špidlík studied the *Philokalia* and the global reach of the philocalic movement in great depth. He was himself profoundly influenced by philocalic spirituality, which found its way into much of his literary output. Under the entry for *Philokalia* in an encyclopaedia of spirituality, Špidlík summarised the book's early history and highlighted some of the differences between the various editions. Theophan the Recluse, for example, omitted certain texts that were apparently too difficult for him, and added others, "expanding on ascetical and moral themes . . . [with] additions from Ephrem the Syrian, Dorotheus of Gaza, and Theodore the Studite."[143] Theophan also took issue with the psycho-physical method (more of which later), felt there was too much theorising about prayer, and dismissed certain physical practices. He thus shortens the extracts from Pseudo-Symeon and adds a critical commentary.[144]

The literary world of Venice played a key role in the publication of the Greek edition. Nicodemus the Hagiorite had already published, in Venice, various works on the spiritual life, including Greek translations of *The Spiritual Exercises of St Ignatius of Loyola* by the Italian Jesuit Giovanni Pietro Pinamonti and *The Spiritual Battle* by Lorenzo Scupoli. The editor of the *Philokalia* thus had access to some of Western Christendom's most important works on spiritual experience and the inner life. The beginnings of an encounter between Eastern and Western spirituality are just discernible, therefore, in the very roots of the philocalic movement.[145] Having mentioned Pin-

---

142) See the entry for "Filocalia," in *Dizionario Enciclopedico di Spiritualità*, ed. Ermanno Ancilli (Rome: Città Nuova, 1990), 1013–1014.

143) Russian idea, 286.

144) Ibid., 292–293.

145) Tomáš Špidlík, "La Filocalia. Annotazioni su un'opera classica della spiritualità orientale" [The Philokalia: An introduction to a classical work of Eastern spirituality], *Rivista di Vita Spirituale diretta dai Padri Carmelitani Scalzi* 41 (1987): 55.

amonti's book on Ignatian spiritual exercises, the question logically arises as to how much, if at all, the instructions in the *Philokalia* resonate with the spiritual practice of the founder of the Society of Jesus. A Jesuit himself, Špidlík recognised clear parallels between the philocalic teaching on *apatheia*, the state of inner freedom, and the Ignatian concept of *indifference*, which also describes a free choice, but in terms of one's spiritual goals. In his book on Ignatius of Loyola and Eastern spirituality, Špidlík describes Hesychasm as offering a practical route to inner peace, but notes that this sense of inner equanimity is also taught by Ignatius: "Like the Desert Fathers, Ignatius goes beyond a purely theoretical framing of life to provide practical advice born of personal experience."[146] In the third of Ignatius's "Three Methods of Prayer," the focus is on breathing, inhalation and exhalation, just as it is in the "Jesus Prayer," as we discover in the Russian work *The Way of a Pilgrim*, which popularised the use of the psychosomatic method outlined in the *Philokalia*. The Ignatian focus on seeking God's will and the emphasis on feelings become, in the *Philokalia*, the spirituality of the heart.[147]

Špidlík refers often to the *Philokalia* in his four volumes of *The Spirituality of the Christian East*, especially in his explorations of Greek and Byzantine spiritual literature. In volume one, the *Systematic Handbook*, he draws on the *Philokalia* in his exposition of the names of Christ and the veneration of Christ.[148] In volume two, *Prayer*, he uses the *Philokalia* to explore two possible approaches to introducing believers to a life of prayer: the first compiles the teachings of the Fathers without commentary; the second, very much in the style of Ignatius Brianchaninov, interprets and explains the classical texts and develops a new synthesis of the principal teachings. Špidlík followed this second path, and inspired by the Hesychast tradition presented his readers with just such a synthesis of the spiritual life. He describes the *Philokalia* as the inspiration behind the revival of Athonite Hesychasm and recalls the two key contributions made by Russians: the editorial work of Paisius Velichkovsky, and the translations from Greek into Russian by Ignatius

146) Ignatius of Loyola, 42.
147) Ibid., 62–67.
148) *Systematic Handbook*, 34–39.

Brianchaninov and Theophan the Recluse.[149] The *Philokalia* informs Špidlík's discourses on the heart—purity of heart, guarding the heart, attentiveness to the heart, the thoughts, desires and resolutions of the heart, the prayer of the heart, revelations of the heart, and divine presence in the heart[150]—and on Hesychasm as the path to continuous inner prayer, particularly his descriptions of the history and practice of the Jesus Prayer.[151]

In volume four, *Monasticism*, Špidlík refers to the *Philokalia* in connection with the struggle against evil thoughts—how they penetrate the heart, and how to discern and be rid of them[152]—and the importance of liturgy in monastic spirituality, especially the contemplative and sacramental aspects:

> If Hesychasts sometimes refrained from a communal celebration of the liturgy, by this they sought to remind us that the ultimate aim of all liturgy is the liturgy of the heart. As Gregory of Sinai said, "A true sanctuary, even before the life to come, is a heart free from distractive thoughts and energised by the Spirit, for all is done and said there spiritually." The whole of the *Philokalia* speaks of this journey from visible liturgy to mystical contemplation[153] . . . and according to the *Philokalia*, contemplation is an "instrument of deification."[154]

The Influence of the Philocalic Movement

In *Ruská idea*, Špidlík describes the prevalence of Hesychasm in pre-*Philokalia* Russia, where the natural environment, especially the profusion of caves and the sheer remoteness of much of the terrain, provided ideal conditions for the monastic life. Among the many fifteenth- and sixteenth-century documents at the Trinity Lavra of St Sergius, researchers uncovered a great number of Hesychastic writings by authors such as John Climacus, Dorotheus of Gaza, Isaac of Syria, Symeon the New Theologian and Gregory of Sinai.[155] Špidlík

149) *Prayer*, 13-14.
150) Ibid., 248.
151) Ibid., 331-332.
152) Monasticism, 160-161.
153) Ibid., 196-197.
154) Ibid., 207.
155) Russian idea, 285.

also noted the influence of Nil Sorsky, who came into contact with Hesychasm during a stay at Mount Athos at the end of the sixteenth century. The Hesychast movement came close to disappearing in Russia, however, and had to wait until the end of the eighteenth century for a revival.[156]

For Špidlík, the philocalic movement started with "the great discovery of beauty in documents that appeared to have been long forgotten, buried deep in the libraries of monasteries no longer in use."[157] This discovery of writings whose authors marvelled at beauty and goodness came at a time when monastic life was in serious decline and society was at its most antipathetic towards the monasteries. In the eighteenth century, monks living under Turkish rule found themselves in a struggle for their very survival, and the secularised Russian imperium was closing monasteries daily. This, however, was the very time that revival came: "It often happens," Špidlík noted, "in the history of monasticism that a new push forward comes precisely at a time of the greatest decadence."[158] The thirteenth and fourteenth centuries had been a boom period for the Russian monasteries. Decline followed in the fifteenth century, followed by attempts at reformation at the turn of the fifteenth and sixteenth through the endeavours of the conservative Joseph of Volokolamsk and the more progressive Nil Sorsky. The main renaissance of the Russian church came in the eighteenth-century, largely through the influence of Paisius Velichkovsky. Because of a lack of spiritual advisers at the time, Paisius decided to gather together the patristic texts available at Mount Athos and translate them into Church Slavonic. When he came across the Venetian *Philokalia*, he added to the texts and published them as the *Dobrotolubiye*.[159] As we have already noted, the Greek text was later translated, twice, into modern Russian through the work of Ignatius Brianchaninov and Theophan the Recluse.[160] Through other translations, the new and thriving philocalic movement soon spread to Romanian and Slavic monasteries, and beyond.

156) Ibid., 286.
157) La Filocalia, 58.
158) Ibid., 55.
159) Ibid., 56.
160) Ibid., 58.

Perhaps the key contribution of the philocalic movement to the Russian spiritual renaissance was its emphasis on prayer, the power of the name of Jesus, and the psycho-physical method. To avoid becoming distracted and exhausted by a plethora of fragmentary thoughts and ideas, the Desert Fathers had sought a way of expressing the affect in their hearts in as few words as possible,[161] seeking the shortest formulation of a prayer that would nonetheless clearly and adequately reflect their inner disposition. They eventually arrived at what we know today as the Jesus Prayer: "Jesus Christ, Son of God, have mercy on me"; the Russians added, "a sinner." The Jesus Prayer is perhaps the most distinctive expression of the philocalic movement and one that reached a broad spectrum of Russian society:

> The Jesus Prayer has been established in monasteries as daily prayer since the days of the philocalic renewal; it has also been offered to the laity. Theophan Zatvornik also believed it could be used with spiritual beginners, as the goal of asceticism is to purify one's heart and spiritualise it; the Prayer of Jesus, says the author, contains both these elements.[162]

The Western world came to know the philocalic movement in its Russian expression largely through *The Way of a Pilgrim*, the book that introduced generations of readers to the psychosomatic method of inner prayer, particularly the Jesus Prayer. In his introduction to the Italian edition, Špidlík reflected on the book's spiritual background, covering such subjects as continuous prayer, maintaining a healthy inner disposition through the use of a short prayer such as the Jesus Prayer, spiritual struggle (*antirrhesis*), different levels of prayer, the feeling of compunction, the purity and everyday nature of prayer, the symbolism of the body, and the physical method as used by the book's protagonist, Pilgrim. He finished on a cautionary note, pointing out that pilgrimage is both hard work and a gift, "a victory over time and a liberation from the cares and concerns of daily life."[163] Pilgrim, who longs to find a place of continuous

---

161) La Filocalia, 65.
162) Russian idea, 289.
163) Tomáš Špidlík, "Introduzione," in *Racconti di un Pellegrino Russo* [The way of a pilgrim] (Rome: Città Nuova, 1997), 7.

prayer, thus belongs to the Russian *straniki*, or seekers after inner peace.

Špidlík wrote prolifically on the history of the search for continuous prayer: the Messalians refused to work that they might devote themselves to prayer, and were criticised for doing so by Augustine; the Acemites from Constantinople were believed to go without sleep in order to be in constant prayer, but in fact their day was divided into three parts, work, rest, and the office, so that at any time of day or night there was always someone at prayer. In Russia, the emphasis in prayer was on the power of the name of Jesus. The *Imiaslavie* movement, whose followers worshipped the name of Jesus, caused something of a stir in the Russian church around 1912-1913. Špidlík generally avoided such controversies, however, and simply explained how for early Christian authors the name of Jesus was associated with the peace of the soul, working as an *antirrhesis*, a means of blocking the *logismoi*. Here Špidlík refers to Evagrius's *Antirrheticos*, which the author divided into sections according to the eight vices.

As he experiments with the Jesus Prayer, Pilgrim also discovers *apatheia* in his body, which occurs when prayer becomes a state of being (*katastasis*) in which the pray-er becomes a prayer. He also experiences a state of constant penitence, like Saint Thalelaeus who spent sixty years of his monastic life weeping over his sins—although Špidlík sees his tears as those which "generate joy."[164] Repentance and prayers of penitence such as the Jesus Prayer lead to a peaceful heart even amid the everyday concerns of life; when this happens, prayer has truly become continuous. Basil the Great, Tikhon of Zadonsk and Pilgrim all occupied themselves, their inner lives, Špidlík suggests, with "living the everyday" in the presence of God. The antinomy between a life lived in the world and a mind lifted into the presence of God was tackled in various ways, and here Špidlík again quotes Saint Basil, who wrote that "all visible things remind us of who is our Benefactor" (*Hexaemeron* 3:10). But pure prayer requires a pure heart, and a pure heart can only be attained through a threefold transformation: first moral—avoiding sin; then psychological—focusing on the words of the prayer without

164) Ibid., 20.

distraction; and finally, in the Evagrian sense, intellectual—experiencing the "pure divine light" in the "bare intellect," unburdened by notions, images and forms. Now all bodily actions and functions become part of the prayer, the gestures and postures a sacred language of their own.

On the physical method itself, Špidlík observes that "despite often referring to the *Philokalia*, the method of the Russian pilgrim . . . is not identical with what the work teaches."[165] He continues his introduction to the book with an overview of the storyline. Guided by a *starets*, a spiritual guide, Pilgrim learns the Jesus Prayer. Initially, while gradually increasing the number of times he recites the prayer, he concentrates on his lips and on careful pronunciation. The prayer then moves into his mind, and finally descends into his heart and into harmony with his heartbeat. To help them share their experience of the Jesus Prayer, the monks had sought a physical symbol that would express the constancy and permanency of the prayer, and had settled on the heart—both the organ itself and the pulse, the heartbeat. Breathing is a symbol or expression of dependence on the outside world, but in the Jesus Prayer, that dependence is on "the One who is the life of the world in a spiritual sense."[166]

Growing experience in the practice of the Jesus Prayer is often attested to by a feeling of inner warmth, or "seeing" the light that illuminates the whole person from within—from the heart. As Špidlík notes, Eastern writers consider these phenomena "natural," and it would be a serious error to consider them a product of grace or proof of the attainment of perfection in prayer or to identify the "psychological states" that result from the exercise with attaining, or having attained, a "state of prayer." A monk would therefore never practise the prayer without spiritual guidance. Equally, if he focused on the form of the prayer or on the physical method itself, he would run the risk of losing his awareness of the presence of God. In the practical recommendations with which he concludes his introduction, Špidlík encourages those who would seek to follow Pilgrim's example to invoke the name of Jesus and to pray the Jesus Prayer, as doing so will help them reject evil thoughts and make

165) Ibid., 29.
166) Ibid., 36.

them conscious of the universal presence of Christ. He also exhorts Christians to apply themselves to other prayers of the Church, to read the Scriptures, and to find a spiritual guide.[167] In all this, there is no need to be overly cautious:

> We can try something simple even by ourselves. We find somewhere peaceful. Our right hand takes hold of our left to feel the rhythm of the pulse. We find a way of moving, walking to the same rhythm. When we achieve that, we regulate our breathing according to that same rhythm. Finally, without counting our breaths, either in or out, we become one with the words of the Jesus Prayer and adapt them to our own way. We walk like this for fifteen minutes. The experience will teach us how to use this peaceful state for true prayer that on the one hand will be as simple as possible, but on the other will draw together our whole being—soul and body—and we will feel unified within ourselves. And this is exactly what our over-analytical European culture has lost.[168]

Philocalic Spirituality Today

Špidlík felt very strongly that the contemplative tradition of Hesychasm was highly relevant for modern-day believers, but insisted that to avoid an erroneous or syncretistic interpretation it was vital to put across a holistic view of spiritual development.

> If we want to present the value of the *Philokalia* to Christians today, we will need to bring to their attention some of the principal features of Eastern spirituality.[169]

The starting point of Eastern spirituality is anthropological. The human person is a microcosm, an image of God in whose heart God acts:

> The contemplative Hesychast tradition has followed this way down through the centuries: it teaches us to discover the beauty of the world inside ourselves, inside the human heart. Nicodemus the Hagiorite de-

---

167) Ibid., 39–42.
168) Ibid., 41.
169) La Filocalia, 58.

cided to collect the texts most characteristic of this tradition at precisely the time European civilisation was dominated by the Enlightenment, by encyclopaedism, when modern technology was born and promised to turn this planet into an earthly paradise. It was at just this time that Nicodemus sought to awaken the consciousness of those who love inner beauty to the existence of another world.[170]

This "rediscovery" of the heart and the emphasis on purifying the heart from sin and its consequences is central to philocalic spirituality: through penitence and conscious endeavour, the believer sets out on a journey towards a pure heart. Špidlík highlighted three meditative aspects of philocalic spirituality which offer themselves to the contemporary Christian: vigilance of the heart, pure prayer, and the "physical method."[171]

Vigilance of the heart begins with the negative stage of preventing evil thoughts, followed by the positive stage of actively guarding a pure heart, which becomes a "wellspring of revelation,"[172] a source of peace and tranquillity, a place where the praying Christian listens to the voice of God, is led by divine inspiration, and contemplates the holy mysteries. The "physical method" of the Hesychasts—which Špidlík once called "Christian yoga"—involves banishing evil thoughts through a different way of thinking. Christ's response to every suggestion of the Evil One with a word of Scripture becomes Evagrius's *antirrhesis*, in which evil is banished by the power of the name of Jesus through use of the Jesus Prayer.

In an extract included in the *Philokalia*, Nikephoros of Mount Athos made recommendations for bodily postures in prayer and gave instructions on the practice of "guarding the heart" from temptation. Using Evagrius, the monk described three kinds of prayer: first, that which fills the mind with divine thoughts and heavenly images but which carries the risk of developing into fantasies, illusions, madness and even thoughts of suicide; second, that which withdraws from the senses and focuses on thinking and conscience—this is exhausting, however, and success can open

170) Ibid., 60.
171) Ibid., 62–70.
172) Ibid., 62.

the door to pride; and finally pure prayer, which is accompanied by "seeing" the divine light.

Pure prayer excludes all forms and concepts; it is immeasurable, incommunicable, like Moses' experience of the burning bush, which transcended any kind of concept. But mystical experiences are generally communicated in a way that enables us to grasp them, usually through a created or sensible object which assumes the status of a symbol, just as the bush that burned without burning up became a symbol of seeing the presence of God. Špidlík always concluded his meditations on philocalic spirituality by noting the possible dangers of practising the Jesus Prayer—the wrong turnings one can take. If a person's moral life fails to match up to their assumed level of advancement in the Jesus Prayer, there is a real danger of spiritual schizophrenia.[173]

The spread of philocalic spirituality was undoubtedly assisted by the translation of the *Philokalia* into other languages: first Church Slavonic and Russian, and later Romanian, Italian, French and Arabic. In an article on the Italian translation, in which he introduced philocalic spirituality and its central theme of prayer to a mostly Catholic readership, Špidlík pointed out the similarity between the approaches to prayer in the Western mystics and spiritual writers and those in the *Philokalia*. Philocalic spirituality insists that prayer is not merely an act but something that takes place within the very essence of human being, as had already been suggested by Origen, Augustine and Thomas Aquinas, and practised by Francis of Assisi. "Who teaches us such prayer?" Špidlík asks. It is the "holy neptic Fathers," those tranquil ones who practised spiritual *nepsis* (watchfulness) and taught those suffering from psychic disquiet how to overcome it and find spiritual peace. Such inner peace, *hesychia*, gave its name to Hesychasm, whose adherents sought a state of continuous prayer and tranquillity. From the Egyptian desert, via the monks of Mount Sinai and their influence on the spirituality of the patriarchate of Constantinople, and later the monks of Mount Athos, we eventually arrive at the publication of the *Philokalia* and the renewal of the spiritual life of the Church.[174]

---

173) Ibid., 70.
174) Tomáš Špidlík, "La Filocalia dei 'Santi Neptici' in italliano" [The Philokalia of the 'Holy Neptics' in Italian], *La Civiltà Cattolica* 137 (1986): 260.

Špidlík wrote of the possible pitfalls in the practice of philocalic spirituality and its many demands on the modern seeker. Referring to the present-day interest in icons, he reflected on the question of imagination in the spiritual life. The Evagrian texts in the *Philokalia* speak very little about image or imagination, and when they do they are somewhat negative, iconoclastic even. Špidlík found more fertile ground in Theophan the Recluse, who translated and promoted the *Philokalia* but also contemplated the beauty of creation. The contemplation of icons and images must begin with a "fasting of the eyes," that is, a fasting from profane images. The ability to see a transformed world comes not at the beginning of a spiritual journey of faith and holiness but at the end, after the purification of the heart.[175] This fasting is from concepts as well as images. It is an apophatic way of knowledge, an approach which Špidlík suggests is "rarely comprehensible" to the modern-day believer.[176] To reject everything visible and sensible, to renounce even one's own thinking and opinions, runs counter to the contemporary mentality, which is why to practise the prayer of the heart the Christian must develop profound self-knowledge.

> The ability to accept the limitations of one's own thinking, even if it is noble, to discover God above ideas, even when they are most devout, is undoubtedly a discovery the modern believer has to make. And if the practice of the simple prayer of the heart leads that person in this direction, it is worth encouraging.[177]

But it is the plea for mercy in the Jesus Prayer which most clearly challenges modern thinking. To achieve an attitude of sincere contrition, the penitent must avoid two equally un-Christian tendencies: either to focus so much on sin that forgiveness becomes almost impossible, or to believe in the ability to deal with sin through one's own strength. These tendencies lead the modern believer either to fear thinking about sin or to avoid it altogether. But in philocalic

175) See Tomáš Špidlík, "L'attualità della Filocalia oggi" [The relevance of the Philokalia today], in Tomáš Špidlík et al., *Amore del bello. Studi sulla Filocalia* [Love of the beautiful: Studies in the Philokalia] (Magnano: Qiqajon, 1991), 13–14.
176) Ibid., 14.
177) Ibid., 15.

spirituality, believers "remain conscious that they are sinners whom God has forgiven."[178]

Finally, Špidlík asked whether practising philocalic spirituality leads to an unhealthy focus on ourselves and whether we would not be better off concentrating on external practices rather than on the inner perfection of the heart. He wisely noted, however, that because "any thoughts we do not control will control us,"[179] we need to practise "the discernment of spirits" and the guarding of the heart, which we can learn through the psychosomatic method of the Jesus Prayer.

Although the *Philokalia* may not appear to be in line with modern thinking, it does in fact address our deepest needs and everything for which we unconsciously thirst:[180]

> Today, more than ever, human beings have a hankering for inner peace and are searching for someone who will offer them a way to unite all the powers of their souls and bodies which are distracted by so many external stimuli and beset by so much unrest. Certainly, modern doctors and psychologists can hold our hand, and their help should not be underestimated. It is only the neptic Fathers, however, who can fill us with trust, so that by the grace of God, we will be able to overcome everything that troubles us, everything that is a consequence of sin. Not in vain did Christ present us with the ideal of the pure heart that is able to see God (Mt 5:6), and in God, the whole cosmos, and indeed ourselves as enlightened, beautiful and harmonious, that we may enjoy, even in this life, the visions given to the apostles on Mount Tabor.[181]

178) Ibid., 17.
179) Ibid., 19.
180) La Filocalia dei "Santi Neptici," 260.
181) Ibid.

ŠPIDLÍK ON ART: A THEOLOGICAL LAST WILL AND TESTAMENT

Špidlík's theology mapped out the intricate path described by the dialogue between the mystical schools of the Christian East and West. The culmination of this lifelong labour of love was a series of reflections on theological aesthetics in which he explored a possible synthesis of existing knowledge into a new kind of "integral knowledge." For Špidlík, integral knowledge is religious, mystical; it intuitively reveals in the visible world the symbols which transcend that world and point towards the invisible mystery of life. The central place in this new synthesis is taken by beauty.

MYSTICISM AND THE THEOLOGY OF BEAUTY

The mystical view of beauty as a symbol of the truth was one of the final themes Špidlík addressed. His preferred summary of the subject was offered by the Russian filmmaker Andrei Tarkovsky: "For beauty is a symbol of something else. Of what exactly? Beauty is a symbol of the truth."[182]

Špidlík first encountered the theology of beauty as a seminarian in Maastricht, where he would often visit the studio of a newly founded school of fine art.

We used to go and look with great curiosity to see how it was all done. On one occasion, a teacher was marking the students' drawings. He showed me some and asked me what I thought. One was of a girl holding a bouquet. I thought it was beautiful and said so. The teacher told me it was the only one that was going to fail. I was very surprised by this, so he explained. He covered part of the drawing, showing me just a leg, and asked me how old I thought the person in the drawing was. Perhaps about fifteen or sixteen. And how old is her hand? Maybe three. And the face? The shoulders are masculine. Yes, he said, the different parts are all very nice but together they're a hotchpotch. The picture can't express anything; there's no idea there which can convey anything. They're just nice colours and nice little forms. In other words, just typical

---

182) Russian idea, 87.

kitsch. He can draw well, excellently even, but he has to fail because I can't turn out artists like this![183]

Just as modern-day encyclopaedism lacks a central idea, the individual parts of the person in the drawing were all very good but together they failed to convey the idea of the whole, and it is this whole which true beauty should reveal. Špidlík found his solution to the problem in the thinking of Vladimir Solovyev, and his peers and successors, who saw beauty as the unifying idea that drew together the separate discoveries of science, philosophy and religion.

Špidlík made further progress in his exploration of beauty as a student in Florence, where little by little his eyes were opened to the beauty of the world—to visible beauty.[184] When asked who had taught him the meaning of beauty, he admitted to being something of an autodidact: "In this field I am a self-learner, and my privileging of the spiritual sense over the aesthetic is not easily understood by aesthetic critics."[185] For Špidlík, spiritual sense consisted in being able to behold beauty intuitively, and through that beauty to see life in all its fullness: "The higher the reality I am able to see in something, the more beautiful is that which I am looking at. . . . That is the true criterion of beauty. And for a Christian, the most beautiful is Christ."[186]

Špidlík continued to reflect on these and related themes and returned to them in many of his writings, always presenting them in a new context and from a new perspective. His insights have been applied at the art studio at the Centro Aletti in Rome, where the relationship between theology and art is a constant subject of reflection.[187] The new design for the Redemptoris Mater Chapel in the Vatican was based on a theological "blueprint" provided by Špidlík. Here, we will focus on three themes in particular: beauty

183) Tomáš Špidlík, "Záznam přednášky P. Tomáše Špidlíka S.J. o ikonách" [A lecture by Fr Thomas Spidlik SJ on icons], in Tomáš Špidlík SJ, *Miscellanea* (unpublished manuscript deposited in Centrum Aletti, Rome, 2007), 12:92.
184) Ibid.
185) Soul of a pilgrim, 137.
186) Ibid., 138.
187) Richard Čemus, "Aristokrat ducha – Tomáš Špidlík" [Aristocrat of the Spirit: Tomáš Špidlík], *Teologické texty* 5 (2003): 203-205.

as the path to integral knowledge; the manifestation of beauty in a mystical ascent; and the supreme expression of beauty in the light of a transformed human face.

Beauty as the Path to Integral Knowledge

In *Ruská idea*, Špidlík's reflections on beauty appear in the chapter on knowledge. Beauty is therefore seen as a subject of gnoseology, the study of the origins and processes of human knowledge. Here, he follows the Russian view that the truth a person comes to know is always alive, spiritual, intuitive, unifying—and beautiful. To know the truth is to enter into an encounter with life, with living reality, which although full of contradictions is intuitively cognised in its spiritual unity. This intuitive approach, which creates a unity between the subject and object of knowledge, is possible only through contemplation and a relationship of love, and love sees beauty in all things: "Through beauty we come to integral and spiritual knowledge."[188]

Like Solovyev, Špidlík saw beauty as the unifying principle of empirical, metaphysical and mystical knowledge. In a lecture entitled "Art will unite the world," Špidlík again drew on Solovyev, for whom the solution to the gnoseological crisis in European culture was to be found in a new unifying principle from the world of aesthetics. Solovyev used the classic example of carbon and diamonds, which have the same chemical composition but only the diamond is considered beautiful, just as the nightingale's song is deemed enchanting and the mewing of a cat an awful racket.

> Only art that truly creates "the beautiful" is able to perform the role of unifying all human knowledge. An artist is active on all levels: on the empirical level, the level of rational thought, but also on the level of spiritual intuition. From the lower level, beauty points to something higher; and starting from the higher, intuition seeks to embody itself in a lower symbol and make it beautiful.[189]

188) Russian idea, 84.
189) Tomáš Špidlík, "Umění sjednotí svět" [Art will unite the world], in *Omnia autem probate*, ed. Petr Kubín, Mlada Mikulicová, and David Svoboda (Prague: Karolinum, 2005), 365.

In this perspective, beauty is not reduced to mere aesthetics but defined in relation to what is good and true. In the Eastern Christian tradition, and according to the *Philokalia*—"love of the beautiful"— the more one grows in love, the more profoundly one comes to know beauty: "If for scholastic philosophy, 'being' is fundamentally *unum-verum-bonum*, for Florensky and Solovyev this triad is replaced by beauty-truth-goodness."[190]

An aesthetic view of the world is by its very nature spiritual and religious. In his entry on "aesthetics" in a dictionary of mysticism, Špidlík examines its relationship to mysticism, and asks whether the two are in contraposition. His definition of aesthetics draws on that of the eighteenth-century German philosopher Alexander Baumgarten, who saw aesthetics as the perfection of sensory knowledge, the object of which is beauty. For Špidlík, then, beauty makes itself visible to the senses by "incarnating itself."[191] Here aesthetics clearly resonates with Christian mysticism in having to do with "coming to know a hidden reality through an intuition enabled by special divine illumination."[192]

Špidlík notes that while Greek thought stopped at the dichotomy between the visible and the intellectual, Christianity was trichotomic, that is, sensory, intellectual and divine. Christian ecstasy therefore transcends two boundaries: between the sensory and the intellectual, and the intellectual and the divine. Crossing the second of these thresholds can be achieved only with the help of God. Špidlík writes about the notion of aesthetics in Basil the Great, Augustine, Theophan the Recluse and especially in Solovyev, Frank, Ivanov and Florensky. According to these latter—and later—Russian authors, visible objects reveal an idea about the One who transcends all beauty, and thus reveal the divine in creation. Beauty is a universal characteristic of being which can be known only through the illumination of the symbolic meaning behind what is visible.[193] In the context of the conflict between worldly aesthetics and an ascetic

190) Russian idea, 87.

191) See Tomáš Špidlík, "Estetika" [Aesthetics], in *Dizionario di mistica* [A dictionary of mysticism], ed. Luigi Borriello, Edmondo Caruana, Maria Rosaria Del Genio, and Nicola Suffi (Rome: Editrice Vaticana, 1998), 479.

192) Ibid.

193) Ibid., 480.

rejection of the world, Špidlík suggests that in the spiritual life, the "fasting of the eyes" moderates the use of sensible forms and reveals the invisible mystery within them.[194] He also speaks of this fasting in the context of creating a work of art: "The artist who creates a form and multiplies it needlessly, so reducing its 'transparency,' is being prodigal."[195] Artistic form requires the same 'bareness' and simplicity as that expressed by a symbol.

In a work co-written with Marko Rupnik, Špidlík prepares his readers for a new kind of knowledge which is revealed through a symbol whose beauty connects two worlds, the visible and the invisible. The invisible world speaks to the visible through the symbolic nature of an image perceived by the senses. Again, Špidlík speaks about the quality of knowledge so that he might defend the need for a theology of symbol. Theology will not fossilise in a symbol; a symbol is not the truth. On the contrary, recalling Origen, Špidlík suggests that the golden rule of the theology of symbol lies in its continual transcendence: "True gnosis consists in continual self-transcendence."[196]

Finding such a symbol in the visible world is a painful and painstaking undertaking, with many mistakes along the way and the ever-present danger of rushing headlong into an idea or fantasy that bears no relation to the real world. In one of his lectures, Špidlík referred to an example Florensky used from the life of Raphael, who confided in Bramante that he dare not depict the Virgin Mary in her heavenly perfection as his vision of her was purely spiritual and he was anxious not to fall into illusion or fantasy; no woman he could possibly depict would ever match his inner vision.[197] Raphael remained in this painful state until he met a certain girl, probably in Florence, whom he began to paint. When he had finished the paint-

194) Ibid., 481.

195) Tomáš Špidlík, "L'aspetto liturgico sacrale dell'immagine nell'oriente cristiano" [The sacral-liturgical dimension of images in Eastern spirituality], *Studi Ecumenici* 10 (1992): 411.

196) Tomáš Špidlík and Marko Rupnik, *Una conoscenza integrale. La via del Simbolo* [Integral knowledge: The way of the Symbol] (Rome: Lipa, 2010), 89.

197) Tomáš Špidlík, "Umenie prejav Ducha" [Art as an expression of the Spirit], in *Kresťanstvo a kultura* [Christianity and culture], ed. Alena Pitralová and Ivan Rusina (Bratislava: Slovenská národná galéria, 1999), 1:23.

ing, a miracle happened, and "the painted form led him to remember his inner vision and became a visible symbol of the invisible."[198] After his initial experience of an inner vision, a "fasting of the eyes" from sensory objects was necessary until the right person appeared in a simple form—a person whose beauty, in its symbolism, best corresponded to the vision.

Špidlík evaluated a work of art according to the nobility, comprehensibility, and richness of its symbols.[199] Lev Uspensky had suggested that whereas Raphael's *Madonna* portrays nothing more than a beautiful woman, her child and their love, Russian icons draw the viewer into a relationship with the Mother of God and reveal the child's divinity; Špidlík admitted that this explanation "may be doing Raphael an injustice."[200] On the matter of comprehensibility, Špidlík compared the painting of a sunset, where only the artist can say that the setting sun symbolises, say, the sorrow of death, with portrayals of the Eucharist, where the symbolism behind the paten or the lamb is more accessible, more comprehensible. Finally, Špidlík appreciated the richness of the symbolic meaning of icons but conceded that a symbolic vision of the world is necessarily personal.[201]

The Manifestation of Beauty in a Mystical Ascent

Drawing a parallel—one of many—between aesthetics and mystical theology, Špidlík suggested that "we call beautiful that which elevates the mind from what is sensible to a transcendent vision, much as a crystal reflects the light from heaven."[202] Mystical knowledge of beauty therefore requires a new and contemplative way of seeing which perceives the forms of the real word as symbols.

If beauty has some relation to truth and the good, it follows that when knowledge of beauty is attained through love, truth and the good must also be present. Likewise, what beauty is to the good and

198) Tomáš Špidlík, "I colori dell'Invisibile" [The colours of the Invisible], in *I colori della luce* [The colours of light], ed. Marko Rupnik (Rome: Lipa, 2003), 12.
199) Tomáš Špidlík, *Alle fonti dell'Europa. In principio era l'arte* [The roots of Europe: In the beginning was art] (Rome: Lipa, 2006), 18.
200) Ibid.
201) Ibid, 19–20.
202) Colours of the Invisible, 11.

to truth, its opposite, ugliness, is to evil and lies. Špidlík followed Frank in differentiating between divine and demonic inspiration and between free and unfree creative work: whereas divine inspiration always carries a sense of freely chosen co-operation, demonic inspiration denies freedom; it binds, shackles, enslaves.[203] Art, like beauty, can never be free from moral implication or beyond good and evil – it has limits: "Human beings should create only that which they are able to sanctify."[204] Špidlík also asks whether being inspired by the beauty we see in the visible world is an act of grace:

> We need to ask artists, thinkers, geniuses what they think about this. Some may not have had a religious experience of the world in the narrow sense. They may speak of inspiration from a higher power, calling it a "Muse" or "Demon," rather than referring to the activity of God.[205]

And again drawing on Frank, he adds:

> In his or her work of art, an artist seeks to express something infinitely beautiful, immortal, and thus divine. But then comes something important: he or she receives an inspiration, identifies with it, and enters into the discernment of spirits.[206]

The discerning of spirits plays an important part in determining the nature of an artist's inspiration: is it an intuition of beauty that leads to transcendence, or the opposite kind of "beauty," narcissistically closed off within itself and cut off from spiritual life?

As someone who taught spiritual theology, especially the theology of the Christian East, Špidlík had a special appreciation of the world of icons and saw within iconography "an ever-present idea of the mystical."[207] In order to recognise the beauty in a symbol and

203) Tomáš Špidlík, "Il culto di Maria nella Chiesa Orientale" [The cult of Mary in the Eastern Church], in *Maria, 'Unica Cooperatrice alla Redenzione'. Atti del Simposio sul Mistero Corredenzione Mariana, Fatima, Portugal, 5-7 May 2005* (New Bedford, MA: Academy of the Immaculate, 2005), 102.
204) Ibid.
205) Ibid., 101.
206) Ibid.
207) Russian idea, 301.

capture it in a work of art, an iconographer must undergo a process of spiritual maturation. In this regard, Špidlík compared the iconographer's work to that of Moses.

> A praying people sanctifies icons and thus makes them "miraculous." But the artist who writes them achieves for those people what Moses achieved for the people of Israel. He helps them on their difficult journey, which according to the classical theology of contemplation involves two challenging steps: first from the sensible meaning to the mental, and thence from intelligible connections to an authentic spiritual vision, to contact with God, to a direct experience of God's presence.[208]

Expanding on these two callings, Špidlík compares Moses' ascent of Mount Sinai—a mystical journey into darkness which nonetheless serves as a model for all spiritual journeys or ascents—and the mystical light in the Gospel accounts of Christ's transfiguration on Mount Tabor. He likewise compares the stages of ascent in Gregory of Nazianzus's mysticism of darkness and Evagrius's mysticism of light. In the former, the first stage is fear, which is the beginning of wisdom – the people heard the power of God on Mount Sinai but were commanded not to set foot on the mountain; the second is knowledge of the truth, which comes through the contemplation of Scripture and creation. The next stage, apophatic theology, admits that no knowledge is capable of containing God as he is "invisible, incomprehensible, unattainable."[209] The final stage is the way of love, in which God makes himself known, and which for Špidlík is where the mysticism of darkness and the mysticism of light finally come together: "If the intellect is the light, then if we leave that light we will find ourselves in darkness. But at the end of that darkness,

208) Tomáš Špidlík, "Teologia dell'iconografia mariana" [The theology of Marian iconography], in *PSV: Parola, spirito e vita, quaderni di lettura biblica. La Madre del Signore* [Word, spirit and truth: Biblical notes. The Mother of the Lord], ed. Carla Burini (Bologna: EDB, 1982), 6:246-247.
209) Tomáš Špidlík, "La mistica ortodossa" [Orthodox mysticism], in *Sentieri illuminati dallo Spirito. Atti del Congresso Internazionale di Mistica. Abbazia di Münsterschwarzach* [Paths illuminated by the Spirit. Proceedings of the International Congress on Mysticism. Münsterschwarzach Abbey] (Rome: OCD, 2006), 371.

even the darkness appears as a yet brighter light, as only love can recognise God-love."[210]

In icons and other Christian images, an experience of love is rendered by the symbol of light. An iconographer is able to capture the beauty in our world only if he or she has had a personal experience of the inner light through which God reveals himself. Such a spiritual vision of beauty is an essential part of a mystical ascent, in which the end of all knowledge is an experience of love. A mystical ascent is impossible without spiritual purification, however. Here, Špidlík again appealed to the mysticism of Evagrius, who suggested that we unite with God through the purification of our minds, which happens, as we have already noted, in three stages: first moral—purification from sin and the passions; then psychological—purification from misleading sensations, fantasies and partial concepts; finally, it reaches the perfect vision of the pure light of the "naked" intellect.[211] This is important from the perspective of the possibility—or impossibility—of capturing and rendering revealed beauty.

To explore the role played by the imagination in spiritual development, Špidlík looked back on the history of the veneration of images and on the origins of the movement against such veneration. Here again he refers to Nikephoros and his threefold model of prayer: the first is based on images of heavenly things and can lead to madness; the second shuns the use of the imagination and can produce tiredness and a lack of mental stability; only the third kind, true prayer, is concentrated in the heart. Špidlík, of course, defended the reverence of beauty and its portrayal in images:

Evagrian teaching plays an important role but it must not be understood in an absolute and separate sense. It represents, let's say, the first level of mysticism, that is, negative, apophatic theology, a living experience with divine transcendence: no human image, no concept can fully express God. Gregory Palamas stated this quite strongly. But as Lossky has rightly insisted, after negation there comes a need for positive

210) Ibid., 373.

211) Tomáš Špidlík, "La creativita artistica nell'origine dell'icona secondo S. Frank e P. Florenskij" [Artistic creativity in the origins of the icon according to S. Frank and P. Florensky], in Il mondo e il sovra-mondo dell'icona [The world and the "world-above" in icons], ed. Sante Graciotti (Florence: Leo S. Olschki, 1998), 7.

completion, and that is achieved by the theology of symbol. Images and concepts regain their value when they become symbols of a higher reality—a reality which transcends them.[212]

Špidlík also drew inspiration from the Russian poet Vyacheslav Ivanov and another threefold model, in this case threefold mysticism: anarchic mysticism, the mysticism of hope, and the mysticism of love. In Ivanov's typology, the beauty of Christ's face is revealed only gradually and according to the level of one's inner illumination. Anarchic mysticism can be seen in Michelangelo's *Last Judgement* in the Sistine Chapel, where mysticism is expressed as the hatred of all evil; here is an image of a youthful soul that is beginning to love the good but fears evil and believes it capable of destroying his soul. The mysticism of hope is captured in Raphael's *Transfiguration*, which provides a vision of the future, of a world which is yet to come, a world to which the disciples are running, up onto the mountain in mystical hope. At the same time they are turning away from a world in which, in the lower part of the painting, the Pharisees, who claim to hate all that is evil, can be seen condemning the woman caught in adultery. The mysticism of love is the final stage of a mystical ascent and this we find in da Vinci's *Last Supper*. Here, in the tilt of his head, Jesus accepts all that is to come as he institutes the Holy Eucharist and through it transforms all there is into perfect beauty: "The true mystic is the one who transforms the world."[213]

Perfect Beauty in the Light of a Transformed Human Face

The Manicheists held that the world of the senses was not created by God and played no part in the work of salvation. But in seeking beauty in the symbols of the sensory world, Špidlík aligned himself with that part of Christian tradition that has always been wholly against the Manichean view, has always appealed to the Biblical message of God's creation of the whole cosmos and always insisted that the sensory world is good and beautiful. Špidlík found this traditional view in, among others, Origen, Basil the Great and John

212) Ibid., 8.
213) Tomáš Špidlík, "Il Volto di Cristo nelle icone russe" [The face of Christ in Russian icons], in *Il Volto dei Volti Cristo* (Gorle: Velar, 2007), 11:124.

Chrysostom, for whom everything on earth exists for the benefit of human beings and enables them to detect, in this world, "the logos (reason) of created things."[214] The beauty of visible things provides its own clue as to who it is that transcends this beauty.

It should be noted, meanwhile, that just as intellectual contemplation is beyond the capacity of the merely human mind, so is the beauty of God not perceived through the human person's aesthetic sense. "God saw that it was beautiful" (Gen 1:10) . . .[215]

Just as in Scripture and liturgical metaphors light is a symbol of divine grace, "an artist's originality is shown," Špidlík suggested, "in the 'illumination of the image,' which is to say, in the way the iconographer is able to illuminate it."[216] In Eastern icons, this light emerges from the subject's inner being, "illuminating the whole person from within, especially the face."[217] Human beings, therefore, made in the image of God, hold a privileged position in the revelation of beauty:

When we think of the human person as an image, that person has beauty, but in varying degrees. The Greek and Latin translations of Genesis 1:26–27, "in God's image and likeness," propose the idea that God first created an aboriginal image—a prototype—and then created human beings according to this image. The intermediate prototype could be Wisdom (Wis 7:26). But the true pre-image according to which human beings were created and through whom they were restored is Jesus Christ, who is "in the form of God" (Phil 2:6); who is the very "image" of God (2 Cor 4:4). There is no doubt that this is the most perfect image imaginable. "Anyone who has seen me has seen the Father" (Jn 14:9), which means that in the visible one we see the most majestic invisible reality: Christ's humanity is the pinnacle of beauty.[218]

In this theological vision, a person's beauty is judged not according to the perfection of external forms but according to the level to

---

214) *Systematic Handbook*, 128.
215) Ibid.
216) Art will unite the world, 368.
217) Ibid., 369.
218) Russian idea, 21–22.

which, in their inner being, they are like Christ. In Christian tradition, the Incarnation reveals perfect beauty, and the most perfect expression of that beauty is the light we see in the face of Christ.

The face is the primary focus of Christian art. The beauty of an illuminated face reveals its likeness to the perfect image of the face of Christ, the face transfigured in the radiant light on Mount Tabor before which his disciples fell to the ground. The beauty of Christ's face is thus the model for the beauty of the faces of the saints who are transformed by and into Christ, and their likeness to Christ is seen most clearly in the beauty of the face. The first assignment for students at one of the painting schools on Mount Athos was to produce, accurately, an icon of the Transfiguration:

> The aim of this test was clear: the student was to demonstrate an ability to contemplate reality through the eyes of the apostles at the moment of revelation on Mount Tabor, that is, spiritually, and to express this vision in paint. Only then can the icon be regarded as sacred and offer our eyes a transformed world and transformed people.[219]

In a lecture at the Pontifical Urban University (the Urbaniana) in Rome in 2007, Špidlík asked whether the image of Christ, or of a saint, in a holy icon can be considered truly authentic. Like others who defend the place of icons in spiritual devotion, Špidlík maintained that an icon's beauty has meaning only in relation to the one who is looking at or praying before it: "Indeed, only believers who love Christ and pray before his image have the capacity to identify an icon made of wood with the person of Christ. The church that blesses and sanctifies icons is doing just the same; an icon no one prays before is no longer sacred."[220] The external form of the face, then, is of only secondary importance to its symbolic meaning. It is this symbolic meaning which a person relates to and comes to know through a relationship of love, which leads in turn to a deeper knowledge of inner beauty. This intuition transcends visible reality

219) Tomáš Špidlík, "La bellezza, via al Volto trasfigurato" [Beauty: The way to the transfigured Face], in *Il Volto dei Volti Cristo* (Gorle: Velar, 2001), 5:27.
220) Tomáš Špidlík, "Dall'immagine alla realta" [From image to reality], in *La Bibbia nelle culture dei popoli* [The Bible in the cultures of peoples], ed. Andrzej Gieniusz and Ambrogio Spreafico (Rome: Urbaniana University Press, 2007), 154.

so is always spiritual. The face is thus a symbol that leads us to the one it represents. The "accuracy" of the depiction is almost irrelevant: reverence for the image, the icon, has to do with a relationship of love with the one depicted, whether the face be an "authentic" reproduction or closer to the mystical vision of its author or the context in which the depiction arose. This is partly why icons that depict the face of Christ or the faces of the saints assume such a variety of forms.

In one of his expositions on the face of Christ, Špidlík recounted the legend of the image "not made by human hand," an image alleged to be a true and authentic imprint of Christ's face. The image, impressed on a piece of cloth, was sent to King Abgar, who on beholding the face was healed of a serious illness. Over the centuries, icons that depict this image have come to differ in how they portray the various features of Christ's face, but this in no way lessens the legend.[221] Under divine inspiration, the authors of such icons sought to capture not merely a perfect copy of the face of Christ but an image that corresponded to their spiritual vision of his beauty.

Let us recap: beauty, for Špidlík, is revealed in the symbolism of the created world and offers a route to integral knowledge. In order to intuitively know true beauty, we must be purified from images that would deflect us from a spiritual vision of that beauty. Such a "fasting of the eyes" comes naturally, however, because once struck by true beauty, the first reaction is to cease finding satisfaction in earthly forms. A spiritual vision appears when we rediscover the symbolic in earthly forms, a discovery which is possible because, as Scripture tells us, the world was created both good and beautiful.

The beauty of the human person stems from the dignity of having being made in the image of God. Perfect beauty was revealed in the person of Jesus Christ, whose transfigured face shone in radiant light on Mount Tabor, and this light has become the model for the light that radiates from the faces of the saints. But the iconographer can only capture this light—the light which revealed the beauty

---

221) Tomáš Špidlík, "Il Volto di Cristo nell spiritualità dei Padri greci" [The face of Christ in the spirituality of the Greek Fathers], in *Il Volto dei Volti Cristo* (Gorle: Velar, 1997), 1:63.

hidden in the world, and which likens us to Christ—if he or she has had a living experience of it.

In this theological perspective, beauty is a symbol of the truth, and that truth is the beauty of the person of Jesus Christ. What kind of beauty is it that will save the world? Only the beauty of the transfigured face of Christ.

CZECH ART AND THE THEOLOGY OF *ANAMNESIS*

Špidlík's interest in Czech art and culture began at an early age. As a student, he was "a passionate reader of Zeyer, and the poets Mácha and Wolker";[222] from the world of classical music, his great love was Dvořák. Špidlík himself wrote poetry, played the violin and took a keen interest in fine art. As a student in Holland, he enjoyed visiting the local art school, and he became still more appreciative of artistic beauty during his novitiate in Florence, where he came to know the Italian masters Fra Angelico and Michelangelo. Finally, in Rome, he had his first encounter with the art of the Christian East:

> After arriving in Italy and spending a year in Florence, my eyes began to be opened, very gradually, to visible beauty. And when in Rome I discovered my interest in the Eastern Church, I understood what Eastern writers meant when they said, "Do not try to prove the truth of the faith with your head—go into a church and look."[223]

For Špidlík, the key to a theological interpretation of art, especially Czech art, was the Russian thinkers, and at the heart of this interpretation was the theology of *anamnesis*, the significance of remembrance, recollection and commemoration, which transcends time and space and makes the past present. Liturgical *anamnesis* culminates in the making present of the events of salvation through the remembrance of the death and resurrection of Christ in the Eucharist, where words, symbolic gestures and works of art combine to make past events real and visible in the here and now.

Anamnesis was partly existential for Špidlík. Unable to return to Communist Czechoslovakia after finishing his studies in Holland,

---

222) Soul of a pilgrim, 137.
223) Ibid., 136.

he expressed his longing for home and the memory of his distant homeland through his reflections on the meaning of Czech art. It was these memories, especially of Czech music and his favourite characters from Czech literature, which were to shape his identity in exile in Rome and provide the inspiration for his theological analysis of the various forms of *anamnesis* and metaphysical nostalgia.

Threefold Nostalgia: A Mystical Interpretation of Czech Baroque

Russian thought not only provided the key to Špidlík's understanding of Czech art but equally helped him reflect on Czech history. He expanded on his interpretation of Ivanov's threefold mysticism by exploring how it could be linked to events from the history of the Czech people, culminating in the arrival of the baroque:

> Ivanov calls the first awakening of religious dynamism "anarchic" mysticism, that is, an absolute "no" to any form of wickedness. Its artistic expression is Christ in *The Last Judgement* by Michelangelo. In Czech history, this attitude was represented by the Hussite soldiers who in the name of truth stood against the rest of the world. But after this anarchic period, Ivanov says, comes the mysticism of hope, represented by Raphael's *Transfiguration*. In our history, after the Hussite wars, the Czech Brethren came singing their vision of a heavenly city, a land of angels lifted high above all the wrath and wars of the world. Ivanov sees the third stage in the face of Christ in *The Last Supper* by Leonardo da Vinci. The Saviour bows his head and says "yes" to the reality of a world which will betray him. It is a mysticism that accepts the Cross, but it is also the renewal of the nation. Is it possible to see this in baroque culture? In a certain sense, yes, in both its purity and its difference.[224]

Špidlík describes how the catastrophes of the first half of the seventeenth century were followed by the renewal of the Czech nation and the arrival of the baroque, whose architecture dressed its Gothic antecessors in an explosion of exuberance and a prolifer-

224) Tomáš Špidlík, "Le principali correnti del barocco ceco" [The main currents in the Czech baroque], in *Storia religiosa dei Cechi e degli Slovacchi* [The spiritual history of the Czechs and Slovaks], ed. L. Vaccaro (Milan: Casa di Matriona, 1987), 122.

ation of saints, exemplified for Špidlík in the statues of Saint John of Nepomuk on Prague's Charles Bridge. Every church had its *regens chori*; joyful Christmas carols were written.

Here Špidlík finds the theology of *anamnesis*, and echoing Ivanov outlines his suggestion of the "threefold nostalgia" of the Czech people: nostalgia for the far away, for the past, and for heaven. During its many wars, the Czech lands had been a crossroads for the armies of Europe, so during the more settled baroque, the Czechs dreamed of distant lands and read about far-off countries. When their suffering was over, they remembered their past and turned to reading historical chronicles. Finally, in their nostalgia for heaven, "the baroque offers mystical direction and authentic religiosity. The heavenly city of which the Czech brethren sang appears afresh as an attractive vision. On every ceiling of the chapels and naves of our churches, one motif is always present: the saint to whom the church is dedicated ascending to the heavens."[225] New churches were often dedicated to the feast of the Ascension of the Virgin Mary, who in numerous images "levitates" between heaven and earth to signify, Špidlík suggests, the proximity of one to the other. Czech theologians Špidlík writes about from this period include Jan Amos Comenius, forced into exile with the Czech Brethren, and his brother in the faith the Jesuit mystic Bedřich Bridel—dubbed the Czech John of the Cross—who wrote classical baroque mystical poetry about heaven and earth meeting in Christ.

Music: Through *Anamnesis* to Higher Knowledge

Špidlík always stressed the importance of broadening one's horizons through an interest in the arts, and suggested that the shortest route to such a cultural awakening was through music.

Sitting one day beside the Minnehaha Falls that had inspired Dvořák to write his ninth symphony, *From the New World*, Špidlík immersed himself in the sounds of the Minnesota countryside and called to mind the musical motifs of the symphony: "Among these motifs we find again and again one highly lyrical motif that is typical Dvořák. It is undoubtedly a returning memory of the far-off

225) Ibid., 131.

homeland, 'my homeland,' the same homeland of which Smetana wrote."[226]

Having received an inspiration for a piece of music, a composer will immediately seek a way of expressing it, will listen to the sounds all around them and recall the musical tones from the places they associate with "home" and which remind them of the people and the stories—both painful and joyful—that have become engrained in their memory. From the original inspiration and the sounds and recollections that follow, the composer creates their symphony.

Introducing a performance of Smetana's *Má Vlast* (My homeland) at the end of a festival of Czech music in Rome, Špidlík spoke of the importance of the beauty of music and of its being an instrument for the salvation of mankind. He acknowledged Wagner's influence on Smetana but stressed that:

> Smetana's music was deeply rooted in the musical tradition of his nation. The piece is called "My homeland," and it is as if we can hear the music of the rivers, the forests and the meadows and in them perceive the joys and pains of the people who lived among them. In the best-known movement, "Vltava," the river's course echoes the dramatic events of human life.[227]

He went on to build a comparison between Smetana's tone poem and Dvořák's ninth symphony, which although inspired by and written in celebration of the New World, provided Špidlík once again with a recurring memory of his—and Dvořák's—homeland.[228]

Babička and Švejk: An *Anamnesis* of Faith and Non-faith

In its ability to evoke memories and bring our past experiences into the present, music has much in common with literary fiction. One of Špidlík's favourite literary characters was the eponymous Babička (Grandma) from the novel by the nineteenth-century Czech author

---

226) Tomáš Špidlík, "Nad Smetanovou 'Mou vlastí'" [On Smetana's "Má Vlast"], *Jezuité* 4 (2004): 7.
227) Ibid., 6.
228) Ibid., 6-7.

Božena Němcová,[229] whom Špidlík always saw as a true patriot and a sincere, if wavering, Catholic.[230] In her recollection of Babička, Němcová somehow managed to express her understanding of the Christian soul. The novel enjoys such popularity among Czechs, Špidlík suggested, because "it depicts our Czech countryside as it was, and the ancient Czech traditions created by our mothers and grandmothers."[231] Špidlík shared his compatriots' enthusiasm for the novel and admired Babička as a woman who "kept the faith" and handed it down to succeeding generations.

> Babička believed in life and everything connected with it, but with her it is eternal life, life in God and in his commandments, in the love that conquers even death. Before she dies she has a dream of Jiří, her long-deceased husband, coming for her. "Barunka read to her the prayer of the dying, she repeating the words after her. Suddenly the lips ceased to move, the eye was fixed upon the crucifix hanging above the bed, the breathing stopped." During the funeral, the countess draws aside the curtain: "When she closed the curtain, she gave a deep sigh and whispered: 'Happy woman!'"[232]

To the countess's exclamation, Špidlík adds: "And happy the nation that holds onto its women and the faith that formed them."[233] This emphasis on a faith passed down by and personified in mothers and grandmothers is fundamental to Slavic spirituality, as Špidlík notes in so many of his writings on the spirituality of the Christian East.[234] "Woman" often symbolises the wisdom that holds together life's contradictions, and embodies and gives form to the love which is grounded in Trinitarian relationships and therefore gives itself freely for others. This symbolism is very clear in the character of Babička, who in all likelihood represents a composite of Němcová's

---

229) Božena Němcová, *The Grandmother*, trans. Frances Gregor (Prague: Vitalis, 2011) (Czech title: *Babička*).
230) Tomáš Špidlík, "'Babička' Boženy Němcové byla věřící žena" [Božena Němcová's "Babička" was a woman of faith], *Nový život* 4 (1963): 4.
231) Ibid., 5.
232) Ibid.
233) Ibid.
234) Russian idea, 335–336.

recollections of her own grandmother and her reflections on the meaning of womanhood.

The theological motif of remembrance, *anamnesis*, the meeting place of eternity and temporality, is especially present in one's memory of people who remained faithful to their belief in eternal life, and Němcová's ideal of Babička as a woman of faith probably came together with the Russian thinkers' intuition of 'eternal womanhood' in Špidlík's memories of his own mother:

> Slavic spirituality is full of God's pilgrims. Such were—and perhaps still are—the simple women of our groves and meadows, and such also was my mother, who with great enthusiasm went on numerous pilgrimages, even though my father tried to spoil it for her as much as he could and reproached her for it in front of others.[235]

Memories of "mother" or "grandmother" often form the basis of a person's inner life and faith. An author, however, also depicts the drama and tragedy of life, the inner struggle between faith and the lack of it, a paradox Špidlík refers to in his comparison of Němcová's Babička and Jaroslav Hašek's most famous character, Švejk.[236] So what did Špidlík make of the eponymous Good Soldier?

In Švejk, Špidlík sees someone who values life only in the here and now and considers all ideologies foolishness, bunkum; Švejk believes in nothing new and takes nothing seriously. He is not simply an egoist, however. Špidlík detects in him an important aspect of the Slavic character, which is "the complete priority of concrete life over any abstract formulation; a respect for reality and a withering criticism of every ideology."[237] Švejk is a cynic, but a respecter of life, which for him means food, drink and friendship. But herein also lies his weakness, for he is a loner, an existentialist who lives a purely ephemeral life. It is his lack of faith, however, which makes Švejk a tragic character:

235) Soul of a pilgrim, 21.
236) Jaroslav Hašek, *The Good Soldier Švejk and His Fortunes in the World War*, trans. Cecil Parrott (London: Penguin, 2005) (Czech title: *Osudy dobrého vojáka Švejka za světové války*).
237) Tomáš Špidlík, "Zamyšlení nad Švejkem" [Reflections on Švejk], *Nový život* 7–8 (1977): 147.

The tragedy of Švejk is that he makes his living as a pedlar of dogs. He does not believe in eternal life. It is a shame Hašek drank himself to death and that he wrote the book so sloppily, little bits at a time. It could have been a tragic book, another *Don Quixote*.[238]

From his careful reading of Hašek's novel, Špidlík picks out an important encounter between Švejk and an old woman: "It is interesting that the only person whom even Švejk cannot bring himself to ridicule is an old grandmother who makes him potato soup and signs the cross on his forehead."[239] Špidlík concludes his comparison of Švejk and Babička with a priest's appeal to his own nation, once again emphasising the spiritual beauty of a person of faith:

If what is truly characteristic of our little Czech person is an existential attitude to life, then there is only one thing that can save him from hopelessness and transform this bizarre caricature into a beautiful living person: faith in everlasting life, faith in the one who came into this world to ordinary little people that they may have life—life in all its fullness![240]

Marian Art and the Calling of the Slavic Nations

The ultimate and most obvious religious expression of the symbol of woman in our memories of our mothers and grandmothers is reverence for the Virgin Mary. In one of his many articles on the pure and perfect embodiment of womanhood in the Mother of God, Špidlík listed some of the key works on the subject from Czech art and culture: Josef Vévoda's poetry collection *Matka Boží v české poezii* (The Mother of God in Czech poetry), published in Czechoslovakia during the First Republic; the work of Jiří Karásek of Lvovice and Jaroslav Vrchlický and their obvious admiration for Mary's beauty, but also Vrchlický's insistence that this beauty was impossible to communicate; the prayers to Mary of drowning sailors; the motifs of the Angelus and the Hail Mary in the work of Svatopluk Čech; prayers for protection in Jiří Mahen's poem; folk sentiments in the poetry of Rudolf Stupavský; the significance of the Immaculate Conception

238) Soul of a pilgrim, 164.
239) Reflections on Švejk, 150.
240) Ibid.

in the work of František Dohnal; the theme of the Annunciation in Beneš Metod Kulda and František Kyselý; Vladimír Šťastný's depiction of the singing of Marian songs on pilgrimages; the motif of Raphael's *Madonna* in Adolf Hejduk; and the invocation of Mary in the poem by Julius Zeyer.[241]

Elsewhere, Špidlík describes the persistence of Marian veneration throughout the history of Czech religious life, beginning with the well-known venerator of Mary, King Charles IV—who established lauds to the Virgin and the practice of bell-ringing when praying the Angelus and was largely responsible for the spread of the cult of the Immaculate Conception—and continuing with the celebration of the Visitation of the Virgin Mary and the Marian images in Stará Boleslav and on the hilltop pilgrimage sites of Svatá Hora and Hostýn.

Naturally, he also refers to Velehrad in Moravia, "the well-known sacred site . . . with its beautiful icon of the Mother of Unity."[242] The icon was an inspiration to Špidlík, and an important symbol of his tireless work for the unity of Eastern and Western Christianity and the "forgotten" calling of the Slavic nations. Špidlík analysed the icon in fine detail, especially what it has to say about the Czech spiritual tradition of ecumenical dialogue, and elaborated on the scenes depicted around the icon's heavy golden frame. In the bottom right-hand corner is a scene from Santa Maria Maggiore in Rome, where the celebrated liturgical writings of Cyril and Methodius were placed on the altar. In the bottom left-hand corner we see Methodius, who taught the first candidates for priesthood at Velehrad. Between these two is a relic of Saint Josafat, a Ukrainian martyr for unity. We also find Clement of Rome, who wrote the first papal letter calling for unity, Saint Joseph, protector of the Church, and various other saints, such as Wenceslas, Ludmila, John Sarkander and John of Nepomuk.[243]

241) Tomáš Špidlík, "Maria v české poezii" [Mary in Czech poetry], *Nový život* 5 (1990): 80–82.

242) Tomáš Špidlík, "La pietà mariana salvezza dei Ceki" [Marian piety: Salvation of the Czechs], in *Maria e la Chiesa del silencio* [Mary and the church of silence], ed. Karlo Balić (Rome: Accademia Mariana Internazionale, 1957), 31.

243) Tomáš Špidlík, "L'immagine della 'Madre di Dio' a Velehrad" [The image of the "Mother or God" at Velehrad], *Immaculata Mediatrix* 3 (2002): 385–386.

Špidlík also speaks of locations in Rome which are connected with Mary and venerated in Czech religious life: the church of Santa Maria in Trastevere with its fresco of the Annunciation and of Wenceslas the Czech prince; the church of Our Lady of Victory, initially dedicated to Saint Paul but re-dedicated to the Virgin following the Catholic victory at the Battle of White Mountain; and the church of Santa Maria Maggiore where Pope Hadrian II granted Cyril and Methodius permission to celebrate the mass after approving the Slavic liturgy.[244] For the Roman exile Špidlík, these sites became places for the remembrance of Czech history and culture and revealed to him his true calling. Špidlík ended his days living very close to the church of Santa Maria Maggiore, and crossed over to eternity to the sound of its bells.

The Theology of Anamnesis in the Work of Otmar Oliva

Špidlík's deep sense of reverence for traditional Czech art was matched by his insistence on the contemporary artist's freedom to adapt to their cultural context—"Be inspired by icons but paint according to the times"[245]—and to seek inspiration from within. Špidlík sought to discover the essence of each artist's unique mode of communication and always appreciated new forms of expression into which modern artists had managed to imprint the seal of the Holy Spirit.

One of the new wave of Czech artists whose work Špidlík interpreted theologically was the sculptor and engraver Otmar Oliva (b. 1952), a native of the Moravian city of Olomouc. Oliva has his studio and foundry at Velehrad, where he works on a variety of objects including liturgical artefacts, bells, gravestones and fountains. Špidlík sees much of Oliva's work as an *anamnesis*, a symbol of the encounter between eternity and temporality, and notes Oliva's genius for creating a line that reflects his search for an artistic form. Oliva's crosses, in whatever medium, often appear to have been carved from gnarled wood that is "about to burst into life with the first leaves of spring."[246] In Oliva's hands, the heavy materials he

244) La pietà, 31.
245) Art will unite the world, 370.
246) Tomáš Špidlík, "Co je krása z hlediska uměleckého?" [What is beauty from the perspective of art], in *Otmar Oliva: Sochy* [Otmar Oliva: Sculptures] (Uherské Hradiště: Slovácké muzeum; Velehrad: Refugium, 1998), 69-70.

works with, whether bronze, lead or marble, become "living wood" or "the smoothest silk." His altars, which seem to require no covering cloth, appear "ready to capture the breeze of the Spirit from above."[247]

A SPIRITUAL-THEOLOGICAL INTERPRETATION OF THE FILMS OF ANDREI TARKOVSKY

Of all those who have reviewed and interpreted the works of the Russian film director Andrei Tarkovsky, Špidlík is one of the few who seemed capable of capturing their hidden religious meaning. This ability was served not only by his erudition and obvious admiration for Tarkovsky, but also by his knowledge of the Russian soul and the theology of Eastern Christians. Špidlík's particular contribution to the discourse on Tarkovsky was to use his unique synthesis of Russian thinking to interpret Tarkovsky's mysticism within a framework of the spiritual themes of Christian theology.[248]

Despite being poorly thought of by some of his own scriptwriters and other Russians in the industry, Tarkovsky was much respected in the West and won numerous awards at prestigious international film festivals. He was born in 1932 into the family of the Russian poet Arseny Tarkovsky. His first feature film, the highly praised *Ivan's Childhood*, narrates the difficult lives of the child soldiers who served as spies in the Second World War. His next film, *Andrei Rublev*, about the life of the fifteenth-century Russian icon writer, and which became a film classic, is a meditation on the meaning of art and how a work of art comes into being. Tarkovsky's enquiry into the meaning of life and the limits of human knowledge is worked out in *Solaris*, a science-fiction film about a planet where a mysteriously intelligent ocean is able to give material form to ideas. *Solaris* was followed by *Mirror*, an autobiographical work full of metaphor, which continually shifts between contemporary scenes and dreamlike flashbacks. The much-praised *Stalker*, in which three men make a hazardous journey into a forbidden zone that reveals a person's hidden desires, explores the themes of crisis, hope and the existential search for meaning. Tarkovsky made his final two

247) Ibid.
248) See Russian idea.

films after emigrating to the West. In *Nostalgia*, a co-production with Italian television, the film's rootless and alienated protagonist searches for the spiritual meaning of life and eventually undergoes a kind of inner purification as he relives his life through a series of memories. Finally, although playing on fears of a nuclear apocalypse, *The Sacrifice* presents a world in which simple acts of faithfulness, honesty and self-sacrifice offer hope and salvation for the human race. Tarkovsky died in 1986.[249]

Špidlík's analysis revealed the spiritual depth of Tarkovsky's films and posed philosophical-theological questions about the tensions human beings experience in the nexus between temporality and eternity. Many passages in the films are difficult to follow on first viewing; a full understanding of certain characters and scenes, and of how the scenes are shot, comes only in retrospect and with knowledge of the meaning behind the whole narrative. Špidlík told me once about an invitation he received to a screening of *Nostalgia*. Many in the audience found the story unengaging and the long scenes boring; some of them even fell asleep. After the screening, however, when Špidlík explained the meaning behind some of the scenes and illuminated many of the subtle details, suddenly everyone wanted to see the film again. If the hidden mysticism—the truth—in Tarkovsky's films is to be revealed in anything like its fullness, it is clearly an advantage to have some kind of theological understanding.

Špidlík compared Tarkovsky to the author Fyodor Dostoyevsky, whose novels are as challenging as Tarkovsky's films despite having been interpreted so many times from a variety of religious and ideological perspectives. Špidlík finds the principal similarity between the two in their anthropological approach to story-telling, a subject much under discussion in the (Catholic) theology of their respective eras:

---

249) For more on Andrei Tarkovsky and his films, see for example, Lyudmila Boyadzhieva, *Andrei Tarkovsky: A Life on the Cross*, trans. Christopher Culiver (London: Glagoslav, 2014); Robert Bird, *Andrei Tarkovsky: Elements of Cinema* (London: Reaktion, 2008); Andrei Tarkovsky, *Sculpting in Time: Reflections on the Cinema*, trans. Kitty Hunter-Blair (Austin: University of Texas Press, 1989).

Tarkovsky is called the poet of film. He is religious in the same way Dostoyevsky is religious. He does not start from religious principles and look at reality from that perspective. His approach is in fact the opposite. He starts from a particular life, from an individual, the way that person is, then seeks solutions to the person's human problems. It becomes apparent that these problems have no solution; that a human being cannot live as a human being unless seen in a deeper perspective.[250]

Špidlík saw *Andrei Rublev* as a treatise on the essence of art and religious beauty and the search for an artistic form following the initial inspiration, and pointed out the possible pitfalls in the artist's search for symbols in the created world. But before we select some images from the film, we should briefly recap Špidlík's view of integral knowledge. In Russian thought, the creative act of coming to know the truth is intuitive, integral, all-encompassing. Russian thinking was wary of making abstractions that bear no relation to the concrete, and held that coming to know the truth requires a relationship with real life. We see this very clearly in Russian art, and especially in iconography. On the one hand, the necessary 'fasting of the eyes' prevents the iconographer from being so absorbed in the created world that it loses its symbolic significance for his or her spiritual growth. On the other, the artist needs a sense of realism, because "one aspect of iconographic symbolism is real forms drawn from concrete life and reduced to their most sober expression."[251]

After the initial inspiration, the artist seeks a form in the created world which will become a symbol that transcends the created. It is this part of the creative process which forms the backdrop to *Andrei Rublev*. Špidlík used two scenes from the film to explain the possible stumbling blocks in the creative process. In the scene entitled "The Holiday," the somewhat aimless monk and future iconographer accidentally sets light to his monk's habit while spying on a naked women at an orgiastic pagan celebration of spring. In the next scene, "The Last Judgement," while the Scriptures are read aloud, Rublev and his assistant are attempting to paint frescoes of

250) Tomáš Špidlík, "Tarkovského film 'Oběť'" [Tarkovsky's "The Sacrifice"], *Nový život* 4 (1988): 65.
251) Russian idea, 304.

the Biblical scene on the walls of the cathedral, but the walls remain resolutely blank.

What was it that Špidlík saw in these scenes that was counter-productive to the creative process? First, in giving in to the sensual and immersing himself in the physicality of a pagan cult, Rublev loses the symbolism behind the physical and with it any possibility of capturing a vision that will transcend the created world. By contrast, in their efforts to give creative expression to a spiritual vision, the monks reading the Scriptures and painting the walls lack the necessary contact with real life which would offer, through its symbolism, the necessary inspiration for a spiritual vision. Špidlík suggests that "a true religious image grows slowly, like the laborious casting of a bell,"[252] and this is eloquently illustrated in the final scene, "The Bell." Špidlík sees the work on the bell as symbolic of the artist's patient search for a religious image and the desire "always to create a work that is in some way eternal."[253] After the initial inspiration, the purpose of the creative process is to capture, soberly, the symbolism concealed within a created object, a symbolism which reveals the intention of the Creator. For an artist, this often requires the acquisition of new knowledge and the painful process of creative rebirth. In this final scene, a prince is searching for someone who will cast him a bell. A young boy lies about knowing the secrets of bell-casting, and Rublev, who has temporarily given up painting, watches as the boy directs the work. When the bell is finally cast, it rings beautifully. In tears, the boy confesses to Rublev that he had lied about his father teaching him how to cast bells. After this confession, Rublev decides to start painting again and asks the boy to become his assistant.

In 1987, Špidlík was invited to a school of cinematography in Rome to present a lecture on the spiritual background to Tarkovsky's films. In line with his theological synthesis of Russian thought, his starting point was the ontological, liturgical and iconographical nature of spirituality.

First, Christian spirituality is ontological: it concerns the totality of human being in its very essence, which in Russian thinking is

252) Tomáš Špidlík, "Andrej Tarkovskij," *Salve* 2 (2004): 46.
253) Ibid.

expressed by the term "person." Špidlík's approach to the ontological dimension of spirituality is likewise personalistic, in that he considered personhood to be at the heart of the encounter between temporality and eternity, the human and the divine. This notion was completely central to Russian thought: "A person is unique, and in its uniqueness is undefinable and unknowable,"[254] and so "we are able to create a symbol of a fundamental characteristic of a person, a sign, a word, which we then insert into a system of other words without providing a definition."[255]

To understand the mystery of a particular person, we require a symbol which is equally particular, or real or concrete, but which also transcends that person. The mystery is then revealed in love and is free from any kind of fatalism. Although this creative freedom leads to inner transformation, there resides in the heart of every person "an invisible struggle behind the screen of semblance."[256]

It was this "person," and especially this person's hope, that Špidlík sought, and found, in Tarkovsky's films. Personalism runs through Tarkovsky's oeuvre like a golden thread. In Russian tradition, the ability to unite the opposites within a person is primarily the gift of the woman, the mother, as we see in *Ivan's Childhood*, which portrays the young protagonist's memories his mother, a woman who was able to bring together into a comprehensive and comprehensible whole the antinomies of life.[257] The film opens with Ivan floating through the idyllic countryside on a beautiful summer's day. When he sees his mother, he runs to her, kneels down and drinks from the bucket she had been carrying, but as he looks up to speak to her the scene is suddenly interrupted and we realise this has all been a dream. Ivan, who is still a child but now a spy in the Second World War, is hiding out in an old windmill and is woken from his reverie by the sound of gunfire. In the midst of this hostile world he continues to dream about his mother and about speaking with her by the well. In one dreamlike sequence, as he looks up

254) Russian idea, 20.
255) Ibid., 23-24.
256) Ibid., 236.
257) Tomáš Špidlík, "Lo sfondo religioso del cinema di Tarkovskij" [Religious violence in the films of Andrei Tarkovsky], in Andrei Tarkovsky, *L'Apocalisse* (Florence: Edizioni della Meridiana, 2005), 49.

from the bottom of the well, his mother is shot and killed. Ivan had in fact seen his whole family murdered by the Germans, an experience which had precipitated his unwitting arrival into adulthood. The mother who appears to the young man in his dreams therefore brings together within herself, within her person, both the joys and the pains of life.

We find the same theme of temporality and eternity, of the living meeting the dead, in *Solaris*. Here, Špidlík suggests, the narrative is a metaphor for a meeting between the earthly and the heavenly. In the film, a psychologist, Kris, is transported to a space station which is orbiting and researching the ocean-planet Solaris, and there he encounters a strange world where the dead appear to come back to life. The water on the eponymous planet apparently has the ability to turn memories into reality, and Kris has a repeated vision of his late wife who has mysteriously come back to life. This is because, Špidlík says, when a person is lifted out of deathly hatred into the kingdom of love, "he discovers that love makes everything alive again."[258] Anyone familiar with Špidlík's work will know his emphasis on co-operation, on *synergeia*. Human beings are free: they are not passive receivers of the Spirit but are called into creative collaboration with God, with his power, with his energies, and "however imperfect this co-operation may be, it is not to be deemed insignificant."[259] In *Solaris*, the human co-operation in view is between the living and the dead, who through death pass painfully from temporality to eternity. Here again is the Russian ideal of *sobornost*,[260] of human co-existence in which the unification of many into one, into "symphonicity," also includes our relationship with the communion of saints, the departed, a relationship that is considered "very personal indeed, intimate even."[261] Špidlík used this theological motif to suggest that Kris continues to remember and encounter his dead-alive wife because the living and the dead travel together on the same purifying journey towards resurrection.

Personhood is closely related to the matter of freedom, a theme which Špidlík suggests is central to Russian spirituality, where it is

258) Andrei Tarkovsky, 2004, 46.
259) Russian idea, 41.
260) Ibid., 120.
261) Ibid., 132.

both metanomical—"it detests being limited by power"[262]—and met-alogical—"it is not confined by the chains of logic."[263] In *Mirror*, the concept of enslavement is seen most powerfully in the scene where Maria—the mother of the protagonist, Alexei—runs back to the printing press where she works as a proofreader to search through some of her recent corrections. She tells a colleague she thinks she might have made a mistake and the colleague too becomes anxious. Maria searches desperately for the offending manuscript, finds what she is looking for and checks the text. Having reassured herself that the word is written correctly, she calms down and begins to laugh at herself. As she walks past a noticeboard on her way out of the print room, we glimpse a poster of Stalin. Here, Špidlík suggests, Tarkovsky is showing us the cause of the suffering of a people condemned to a life of constant correction and adaptation to new norms. Seeking the truth about people, however, means "seeking a spiritual necessity in a multitude of expressions that cannot be confined within any one system."[264]

Freedom is first and foremost a spiritual matter. And, as Špidlík adds in a reference to the film *Stalker*, "it is necessary to reach the free Zone and avoid being seen by those who control it."[265] Searching for the meaning of life, the three lead characters in *Stalker* set out for a mysterious "Zone" which is closely guarded by soldiers who shoot intruders on sight. Only when the men manage to free themselves from the soldiers are they ready to search for the truth about life in terms of external freedom. First, however, in this zone that offers new and life-changing experiences, they must rid themselves of their inner enslavement.

The second, liturgical aspect of spirituality relates principally to memory, remembrance and eternity. In liturgy, remembrance has to do with memories which transcend temporality, and the fullest expression of this is the liturgical *anamnesis* of the Eucharist.[266] Russian thinkers perceive eternity not merely as an infinite period of time, or as the "inert motionlessness" of philosophy, but as the

---

262) Ibid., 28.
263) Ibid.
264) Tomáš Špidlík, "Andrej Tarkovský," *Nový život* 3 (1987): 32.
265) Religious violence, 47.
266) Russian idea, 311.

liturgical mystery of the life of Christ. As we have already noted, these themes of memory and eternity are seen very clearly in *Solaris*, but *Nostalgia* also explores the relationship between the two. The main character, the writer Andrei Gorchakov, an émigré from his wretched existence in Soviet Russia, finds himself in "heaven" among the crumbling architecture of Italy but soon tires of all the sightseeing and the beautiful works of art. In an opening scene, we see a group of women processing through a crypt carrying a Madonna. Gorchakov's travelling companion, the beautiful Eugenia, is visiting the crypt and asks the sacristan why women always appear more religious than men. She then watches as one of the women kneels down to pray before lifting the Madonna's robe and releasing a flock of small birds. In the following scene, shot in black and white, Gorchakov picks up a white feather which has fallen to the ground. Later, he meets a strange character called Domenico, who presents Gorchakov with a small candle and asks him to take it to the pool at the spa as the villagers will not let him do it himself. Špidlík suggests that the eccentric Domenico—who claims to converse with Saint Catherine and once held his family captive for seven years to save them from the end of the world—is the archetypal fool for Christ, well known in Russian spirituality as the *yurodivy* or holy fools, who unmask every hypocrisy, even, or perhaps especially, among the respected members of society. Such "fools" make frequent appearances in Tarkovsky's films:

> In *Nostalgia*, there is the fool Domenico, who inspires Gorchakov to embark on an adventure of faith. In *The Sacrifice*, it is Maria who shows these signs of ignorance, or folly. A holy fool shows the true path, not because of what he or she thinks or says but because he or she can see what others cannot see. In Russia, this view is so prevalent that many saints are numbered among the *yurodivy*.[267]

It is towards the end of the film that we encounter the liturgical aspect of spirituality. First, we see Domenico immolating himself, apparently for the eternal ideal of *"Zoe! Zoe!"* (Life! Life!), or, as Špidlík suggests, for an abstract idea. After Domenico's "sacrifice"

267) Religious violence, 52.

there follows a scene in which Gorchakov lights the candle Domenico had given him and in fulfilment of Domenico's request proceeds to walk slowly across the now empty pool at the spa. Every time the wind extinguishes the candle he lights it again and repeats his journey to the far side of the pool. Eventually he places the candle carefully on a ledge but immediately collapses, all to a soundtrack of the Byzantine funeral hymn the *"Vichnaya Pamyat"* (Eternal memory). Špidlík sees this scene, and the next, in which Gorchakov has a brief flashback to his childhood, as an image of the relationship between eternity and temporality.

> It is no accident that the *"Vichnaya Pamyat"* is sung during the Byzantine funeral liturgy. All the good we experienced in our life of faith enters into "God's memory" and becomes eternal in God.[268]

For the Russians, "eternity is not the opposite of time . . . it is its recapitulation, an *anamnesis*."[269] Time as a succession of individual moments in a person's life is transcended in the mystery of that person. It is now clear why Špidlík was interested in Gorchakov's replaying of a scene from his childhood after his final collapse at the spa: his spirituality becomes liturgical as eternity enters his memories and everything suddenly comes together. Through faith, a worldly man's nostalgia becomes a liturgical *anamnesis*.[270]

Finally, Špidlík spoke of the iconographical aspect of spirituality. A true icon cannot be written by a monk who is detached from real life, nor can it emerge from sensible, earthly forms, but only after the iconographer has gained inspiration from and found symbolism in a particular life and has experienced the required inner transformation: "[Even] the image of the Holy Trinity is created only after much suffering and life experience. It is only life and the suffering it entails that will assist us in gaining a true image of eternal life in God, helping us desire it and appreciate its beauty."[271] As we have already mentioned, the final scene of *Andrei Rublev* speaks of purification through pain and suffering, a purification which carries

268) Andrei Tarkovsky, 2004, 46.
269) Russian idea, 310.
270) Andrei Tarkovsky, 1987, 33.
271) Ibid.

the presence of the divine, is capable of transforming the world, and is expressed symbolically in "the ringing of the new bell."[272] In a catalogue for one of Otmar Oliva's exhibitions, Špidlík compares the casting of the bell with Oliva's "work with hard materials." Here once again we find Špidlík's ability to see the universal message of art in the creation of a single piece:

> A truly artistic work can be created only out of an experience of pain, but one that brings with it the profound conviction that suffering is not the final word but a necessary preface to the next word, one that proclaims the elemental power of life, which was born out of the soil of the earth but is carried up to heavenly beauty in the sound of the bell.[273]

Tarkovsky's final film, *The Sacrifice*, narrates the mystery and inner struggles of the human person and the sudden presence of unexpected hope even in the midst of a seemingly hopeless situation. In the opening scene, the camera tracks very slowly over every detail of da Vinci's *Adoration of the Magi*. This shot of a well-known work of Renaissance art passes without commentary, but we immediately cut to the film's main character, Alexander, expressing great wonder at each image in a book of icons. This contrast between paintings and icons conveyed to Špidlík the sense of alienation Tarkovsky experienced in Western society and culture. Tarkovsky had no feeling for Renaissance art and insisted that its emphasis on the perfection of the physical form obscured any possibility of spiritual communication.

Alexander, a university professor living on a remote island, teaches his mute son that if the world is to be saved everything must be done properly and in good order, a belief he supports by watering an apparently lifeless tree in the hope that one day it will spring into life. Soon, however, Alexander reveals his fear of the end of the world—a world focused purely on material values. When the radio announces imminent nuclear war, his wife breaks down, has an hysterical fit and has to be sedated. In an attempt to avert the coming catastrophe, Alexander decides to sacrifice all he has and sets light

272) Religious violence, 61.
273) What is beauty? 70.

to his house and all his possessions. Among his friends and neighbours who run to watch the flames is Maria, whom Alexander had asked for help in a dream he had had the night before. Alexander embraces Maria, but an ambulance soon arrives to take him away. The apocalyptic climax to the film is not all gloom, however. While watering Alexander's tree, the mute child, who has since had an operation on his vocal cords, utters his first and only words in the film: "In the beginning was the Word. Why is that, Papa?"

Špidlík's reflections on the film focus on what is symbolic in each of the characters: the sadness of the postman who spends his life collecting stories of inexplicable and semi-miraculous events; the impatience of the doctor who retains a sense of inner calm but ultimately loses control and wants to disappear to the other side of the world; the hope of the mute child; the saintliness of Maria. The inner symbolism of the characters reveals their inner struggles and hopelessness but also a sense of eternal hope: hope in the life to come.[274] The film speaks to Špidlík of Tarkovsky's great compassion on a world heading for catastrophe, and reveals the fundamental human feeling of responsibility towards that world and the desire to make a spiritual sacrifice that will secure its salvation.[275] Just as Špidlík's reflections on art became his own theological last will and testament, so he sees *The Sacrifice* as Tarkovsky's valedictory statement, his final message to the world.

274) Tarkovsky's "The Sacrifice," 65–66.
275) Religious violence, 62.

WORKS BY TOMÁŠ ŠPIDLÍK

Alle fonti dell'Europa. In principio era l'arte. Rome: Lipa, 2006.

"Andrej Tarkovskij." *Salve* 2 (2004): 45-47.

"Andrej Tarkovský." *Nový život* 3 (1987): 32-33.

The Art of Purifying the Heart. Translated by Liam Kelly. Miami: Convivium Press, 2010.

"L'aspetto liturgico sacrale dell'immagine nell'Oriente cristiano." *Studi Ecumenici* 10 (1992): 397-418.

"L'attualità della Filocalia oggi." In Tomáš Špidlík et al., *Amore del bello. Studi sulla Filocalia*, 9-24. Magnano: Qiqajon, 1991.

"'Babička' Boženy Němcové byla věřící žena." *Nový život* 4 (1963): 88-89.

"*La bellezza, via al Volto trasfigurato.*" In *Il Volto dei Volti Cristo*, 5:27-30. Gorle: Velar, 2001.

"La carità degli stazcy: Padre Pio da Pietrelcina e Ioann di Kronštadt." In *Santità e carità tra Oriente e Occidente*, edited by Marco Gnavi, 115-131. Milan: Leonardo International, 2004.

"Čeští jezuité a slovanský Východ." In *Velehrad—filologoi versus filosofoi: Příspěvek spirituální teologie k 800letému výročí*, edited by Michal Altrichter, 245-249. Olomouc: Refugium, 2005.

"Co je krása z hlediska uměleckého?" In *Otmar Oliva: Sochy*, 69-70. Uherské Hradiště: Slovácké muzeum; Velehrad: Refugium, 1998.

"Co pro mě znamená Velehrad?" *Velehradský zpravodaj* 15 (2004): 15-16.

"I colori dell'Invisibile." In *I colori della luce*, edited by Marko Rupnik, 11-12. Rome: Lipa, 2003.

Una conoscenza integrale. La via del Simbolo. Rome: Lipa, 2010. Co-authored with Marko Rupnik.

"La creativita artistica nell'origine dell'icona secondo S. Frank e P. Florenskij." In *Il mondo e il sovra-mondo dell'icon*, edited by Sante Graciotti, 7-17. Florence: Leo S. Olschki, 1998.

"Il culto di Maria nella Chiesa Orientale." In *Maria, 'Unica Cooperatrice alla Redenzione'. Atti del Simposio sul Mistero Corredenzione Mariana, Fatima, Portugal, 5-7 May 2005*, 93-112. New Bedford, MA: Academy of the Immaculate, 2005.

"Cyril a Metoděj: Světci stále aktuální." In *Acta VIII. Conventus Velehradensis Anno 2007*. Olomouc: Refugium Velehrad-Roma, 2011.

"Cyrilometodějská tradice." *Jezuité* 5 (2004): 1-8.

"Dall'immagine alla realta." In *La Bibbia nelle culture dei popoli*, edited by Andrzej Gieniusz and Ambrogio Spreafico, 149-160. Rome: Urbaniana University Press, 2008.

"Duchovní jednota Evropy." *Revue Universum* 2 (2004): 37–42.

Duše poutníka. Tomáš Špidlík v rozhovoru s Janem Paulasem. Kostelní Vydří: Karmelitánské nakladatelství, 2004.

Duše Ruska s Tomášem Špidlíkem. Kostelní Vydří: Karmelitánské nakladatelství, 2000.

"Dýchat oběma stranami plic." *Nový život* 7-8 (2001): 83–84.

"Ekumenismus v CM tradici." *Nový život* 7 (1988): 122–123.

"Estetika." In *Dizionario di mistica*, edited by Luigi Borriello, Edmondo Caruana, Maria Rosaria Del Genio, and Nicola Suffi, 479–481. Rome: Editrice Vaticana, 1998.

"L'Eucatistia – anamnesi dell'eternità." In *Il Volto dei Volti Cristo*, 4:8–10. Gorle: Velar, 2000.

Eucharistie. Lék nesmrtelnosti. Olomouc: Refugium Velehrad-Roma, 2005.

"Filocalia." In *Dizionario Enciclopedico di Spiritualità*, edited by Ermanno Ancilli, 1013-1014. Rome: Città Nuova, 1990.

"La Filocalia. Annotazioni su un'opera classica della spiritualità orientale." In *Rivista di Vita Spirituale diretta dai Padri Carmelitani Scalzi* 41 (1987): 55–71.

"La Filocalia dei 'Santi Neptici' in italliano." *La Civiltà Cattolica* 137 (1986): 257–260.

"L'idea cirillo-metodiana e il messianismu slavo: un 'antinomia originaria'?" *La Civiltà Cattolica* 143 (1992): 431–440.

Ignác z Loyoly a spiritualita Východu. Velehrad: Refugium, 2001.

"L'immagine della 'Madre di Dio' a Velehrad." *Immaculata Mediatrix* 3 (2002): 385–386.

"Introduzione." In *Racconti di un Pellegrino Russo*, 7–42. Rome: Città Nuova, 1997.

K vyšším věcem jsem se narodil. Prague: Alverna, 1991.

Klíč k neznámému. Rome: Křesťanská akademie, 1969.

"Maria v české poezii." *Nový život* 5 (1990): 80–82.

"Matka unie." *Nový život* 3 (1954): 37–38.

"La mistica ortodossa." In *Sentieri illuminati dallo Spirito. Atti del Congresso Internazionale di Mistica. Abbazia di Münsterschwarzach*, 369–384. Rome: OCD, 2006.

My v Trojici. Kostelní Vydří: Karmelitánské nakladatelství, 2000.

"Nad Smetanovou 'Mou vlastí'." *Jezuité* 4 (2004): 6-7.

"Nell'Eucaristia lo Spirito Santo illumina, purifica e unifica." *Potenza divina d'amore* 14, no. 5 (2005): no page numbers.

"La pietà mariana salvezza dei Ceki." In *Maria e la Chiesa del silencio*, edited by Karlo Balić, 29–31. Rome: Accademia Mariana Internazionale, 1957.

Po tvých stezkách. Rome: Křesťanská akademie, 1968.

Prameny světla. Velehrad: Refugium, 2005.

Prayer. Translated by Anthony Gythiel. Kalamazoo, MI: Cistercian Publications, 2005.

"Le principali correnti del barocco ceco." In *Storia religiosa dei Cechi e degli Slovacchi*, edited by L. Vaccaro, 121-138. Milan: Casa di Matriona, 1987.

"Procesí Božího těla." *Nový život* 6 (2000): 102-104.

Ruská idea: Jiný pohled na člověka. Velehrad: Refugium, 1996.

"Lo sfondo religioso del cinema di Tarkovskij." In *Andrei Tarkovsky, L'Apocalisse*, 39-65. Florence: Edizioni della Meridiana, 2005.

"Sofiologie sv. Basila." In Tomáš Špidlík et al., *Od Sofie k New Age*, 10-18. Olomouc: Refugium Velehrad-Roma, 2001.

Spiritualita křesťanského Východu. Vol. 4, *Mnišství*. Velehrad: Refugium, 2004.

The Spirituality of the Christian East: A Systematic Handbook. Translated by Anthony Gythiel. Collegeville, MN: Liturgical Press, 2008.

"Tarkovského film 'Oběť'." *Nový život* 4 (1988): 65-66.

"Teologia dell'iconografia mariana." In *PSV: Parola, spirito e vita, quaderni di lettura biblica. La Madre del Signore*, edited by Clara Burini, 6:243-254. Bologna: EDB, 1982.

"Umění sjednotí svět." In *Omnia autem probate*, edited by Petr Kubín, Mlada Mikulicová, and David Svoboda, 364-375. Prague: Karolinum, 2005.

"Umenie prejav Ducha." In *Kresťanstvo a kultura*, edited by Alena Piatrová and Ivan Rusina, 1:19-27. Bratislava: Slovenská národná galéria, 2000.

Věřím v život věčný. Eschatologie. Olomouc: Refugium Velehrad-Roma, 2007.

"Il Volto di Cristo nell spiritualità dei Padri greci." In *Il Volto dei Volti Cristo*, 1:56-64. Gorle: Velar, 1997.

"Il Volto di Cristo nelle icone russe." In *Il Volto dei Volti Cristo*, 11:11-16. Gorle: Velar, 2007.

Vnitřně zakoušet. Eseje pro duchovní život. Olomouc: Refugium Velehrad-Roma, 2009.

"Východní spiritualita." *Hlas Velehradu* 5 (1993): 177-196.

"Zamyšlení nad Švejkem." *Nový život* 7-8 (1977): 146-150.

"Záznam přednášky P. Tomáše Špidlíka S.J. o ikonách." In Tomáš Špidlík SJ, *Miscellanea*, 12:80-94. Unpublished manuscript deposited in Centrum Aletti, Rome, 2007.

Znáš Boha Otce i Syna i Ducha svatého? Velehrad: Refugium, 2005.

OTHER WORKS

Ambros, Pavel. *Kardinal Tomáš Špidlík SJ - starec a teolog nerozdělené církve. Kompletní bibliografie 1938-2011*. Velehrad: Refugium, 2012.

Bird, Robert. *Andrei Tarkovsky: Elements of Cinema*. London: Reaktion, 2008.

Boyadzhieva, Lyudmila. *Andrei Tarkovsky: A Life on the Cross*. Translated by Christopher Culiver. London: Glagoslav, 2014.

Čemus, Richard. "Aristokrat ducha – Tomáš Špidlík." *Teologické texty* 5 (2003): 203–205.

Dziwisz, Stanisław. "Moudrost srdce." In *Velehrad-Řím. Modlil se tváří k východu*, edited by Pavel Ambros and Luisa Karczubová, 12–13. Olomouc: Refugium, 2010.

Hašek, Jaroslav. *The Good Soldier Švejk and His Fortunes in the World War*. Translated by Cecil Parrott. London: Penguin, 2005.

Němcová, Božena. *The Grandmother*. Translated by Frances Gregor. Prague: Vitalis, 2011.

Rupnik, Marko. *Sarkofág otce Tomáše Špidlíka*. Olomouc: Refugium Velehrad-Roma, 2011.

Tarkovsky, Andrei. *Sculpting in Time: Reflections on the Cinema*. Translated by Kitty Hunter-Blair. Austin: University of Texas Press, 1989.

Karel Sládek is an associate professor at the Catholic theological faculty of Charles University in Prague. He studied physical geography at the faculty of science at the same university, specialising in landscape ecology, and continued his studies at the philosophical and theological faculty of the Pontifical Urban University (the Urbaniana) in Rome. He is a follower of the theological school of Professor Tomáš Špidlík. His fields of expertise are spiritual theology, the spirituality of the Christian East, and environmental ethics, and his interests outside theology include landscape ecology, beekeeping and gamekeeping. He lives in the town of Chrudim with his wife Eva. His numerous monographs and articles include: *Ekologická spiritualita a etika* (Ecological spirituality and ethics), 2018; *Spiritualita a psychosomatika* (Spirituality and psychosomatics), with William Kopecký, 2017; *Na cestě s Jackem Kerouacem* (On the road with Jack Kerouac), 2016; *Včela chrudimská* (The Chrudim bee), 2015; *Ruská menšina a česká společnost* (Russian minority and Czech society), 2014; *Cesty k boholidství* (Paths to divinity-humanity), 2012; *Nikolaj Losskij: obhájce mystické intuice* (Nikolai Lossky: Defender of mystical intuition), 2012; *Mystická teologie východoslovanských křesťanů* (The mystical theology of Eastern Slavic Christians), 2010; and *Vladimír Solovjov: mystik a prorok* (Vladimir Solovyev: Mystic and prophet), 2009.